Single Mom...Slaying It!

An Empowering Resource Guide to Expand Your Superpowers

Andrea M. Pearson

Single Mom...Slaying It!

I dedicate this book to my son Ethan. He is my number one supporter, my accountability partner in getting this book written, and my biggest cheerleader. He is the reason I wake up and hustle every day. He inspires me to be the best possible version of myself, and has been my biggest teacher in life. By completing my life and making me whole, he is most definitely the best thing that has ever happened to me.

My love for books started at an early age. I remember my mom always reading, whether it be at home, in the car, by the pool or at the beach. Many of my childhood memories are of us walking to our neighborhood library together and my mom reading to me. My mom's favorite gifts to my son are gift certificates to Barnes & Noble, which has helped instill a passion for books in him. A love of reading has transcended three generations. My mom is another one of my biggest supporters. I am so appreciative of her love and presence in my life. Thank you, Mom, Rita J. Cottingham, for always being there for me.

Table of Contents

Introduction: You Are Stronger Than You Realize

Supergirl, Catwoman and Wonder Woman Were All Single. Give Them a Messy Divorce and a Kid or Two and See How They Do!

Have you ever wanted to give up? As a single mom myself, I know we've all had those days where it seems like everything, and I do mean *everything,* goes wrong and life is too hard to handle. I've certainly had my share of days where I am completely overwhelmed and feel like a failure. When I was going through my divorce, I either wanted to scream at the top of my lungs or cry myself to sleep many days. Life definitely wasn't easy.

Some days you just don't want to be an adult at all. The struggle, as they say, is *real.*

It would be so nice to fly to an exotic destination and lounge on a white sand beach from dawn 'til dusk, with hot men serving you delicious frozen drinks, am I right? As wonderful as that sounds, the reality of being a single mom is staring you right in the face. But don't worry. You are not alone.

Buckle up your seatbelt and enjoy the crazy ride—I have good news for you. Things are going to get better. A *lot* better. Think of me as your big sister in this journey...I've been there, done that, and lived to tell the tale. I know that what you are going through right now is really hard. I'm not going to sugarcoat things for a newly separated or newly single mother. You're likely facing guilt, financial stress, and maybe even judgment from friends and family. But you're going to be okay, *better* than okay, and I'm going to help you figure out exactly how.

- As you read this book, you'll hear from not only me, but from many single moms who are making it work and creating beautiful, fulfilling lives for themselves and for their children.
- You'll hear from experts, including a financial planner and an attorney, about smart steps to take *right now* to make sure all your ducks are in order.
- You'll learn about amazing support groups and organizations around the country and online you can turn to *today* to find the help or advice you need.
- You'll find out where to turn for additional financial resources to get your family through the roughest patches and ensure your kids have the necessities.
- You'll read tried-and-true tips and ideas for navigating this phase of your life—we'll get into everything from fitness and nutrition to dating and co-parenting—as well as affirmations and encouragement to help you weather the storm. You've got this, Mama.

I wrote this book to demystify negative stereotypes about divorce and single mothers. I wrote it to reduce the stigma that many women feel when they find themselves raising a child or children on their own. I wrote it to provide a sisterhood, to offer community support and to give you an uplifting and inspirational resource. This book has been many years in the making, and I put my heart, my soul, and my most personal experiences and insights into it. I'm sharing it all, so you feel less alone.

I made it through my divorce, and I've been a happy single mother for many years now. No, it's not easy. Yes, I had to cut back on my lifestyle. Yes, it has been stressful at times. I didn't write this book to paint an unrealistically rosy picture for you. This is real life. But you know what? I'm *so* much happier now than I was before. At the end of the day, I am stronger emotionally and more content overall. And you will be, too.

Single Parent Households, by the Numbers

According to the U.S. Census Bureau, there were 12 million single parent families in 2016, with 83% headed by single mothers. Fifty-one percent are either divorced, separated, or widowed, while a whopping 49% have never been married. I honestly had no idea the vast number of children being born to unwed mothers. Nearly two thirds are born to mothers under the age of 30.

Forty percent of children being raised by just their mothers live under the poverty line. Contrast this statistic to the numbers regarding children living with just their fathers: of these, only 21% live in poverty. Interesting. It clearly shows the disparity between income levels. Single moms hold multiple jobs just to survive. Talk about stress!

Today, the traditional household is no longer the norm across the board. Many untraditional families exist, including children from remarriages and multi-partner fertility. There are also couples who cohabitate without being married and have children together. I have been a single mom for five years, and see many single moms struggling to survive. Many of them are in despair and could use some help and motivation. Countless single moms have opened up to me and expressed how isolated and lonely they feel. They don't typically share their worries and stress with others for fear of being judged, yet the numbers do not lie. Single mothers are everywhere, and we need to support one another.

> *You are allowed to feel the way you do. You don't need to explain yourself to anyone.*

I am writing this book both from the perspective of my own experiences as a single mom, and as a coach with many clients exactly like you. The most important part of being a coach is having a strong vision and belief for my clients—holding a vision for my single moms, that their futures will be bright.

I believe, without a shadow of doubt, that you are capable of becoming that future self you're dreaming about. In fact, I know a part of you already is.

A coach holds a big vision for the client even when, and *especially* when, she can't hold it for herself. I want you, reader, to believe in yourself and your future.

- You will get through this.
- You are brave.
- You are strong and capable.
- You are enough.
- You are a great mom.
- You deserve happiness

For those of you who were single moms from day one, I give you many props. That could not have been easy. The amount of work and lack of sleep associated with a newborn is exhausting—to say the least. I completely understand why they use sleep deprivation as a way to torture criminals and captives of war! Under 2% of single parents are widows or widowers, which brings its own set of emotions and challenges. Instead of saying or believing one type of single parenting is harder than the others, we all need to support one another and lose the judgment and comparison. It's not a competition.

While this book is for *every* single mom out there, my main focus is on those mothers who are newly separated or going through a divorce right now. The journey from happily married to happily divorced isn't a short one, and I understand that you did not plan to be where you are in this moment. It might be helpful to keep in mind that your story is not over—not even close. It's just beginning.

Dear reader, I speak from experience. You'll find what you need in these pages to make the next part of the journey a little less bumpy. Read on, my Single Mom Tribe!

> *Divorce isn't such a tragedy. A tragedy is staying in an unhappy marriage, teaching your children the wrong things about love. Nobody ever died of divorce. ~Jennifer Weiner, Fly Away Home*

Chapter 1: Getting Through Your Divorce

It will get better. I promise.

Most people do not enter into their marriage with doubts. It's human nature to squash and deny the existence of red flags. I know many of you have had to endure nasty divorces with a lot of court aggravation. I am sorry if you went through this, or are currently in the process. It might not be easy, but you will make it through. I can assure you, you aren't the first person to get a divorce, and sadly you won't be the last. It takes two people to make any sort of a relationship work, or fail. It isn't fair, or right, to put the entire blame or fault on your partner. You both contributed to the demise of your marriage. It's up to you to be mature enough to realize and accept that. Learn and grow from your past mistakes, otherwise you will continue to bring them into future relationships.

> ***You are not what happened to you,***
> ***you are what you choose to be.***

If you are newly separated from your spouse, your head is likely spinning with questions. The most common ones I see in the Facebook group I run, Sisterhood of Single Moms, include:

1. How will we explain this to the children?
2. What kind of support is there for kids?
3. How do I file for child support? Alimony? Custody?
4. How will we co-parent?
5. How will I find childcare/daycare for children?
6. Are there support groups for parents?
7. How do I file taxes?
8. How do I handle debt? Loans? Marital property? Retirement funds?
9. How will I support us financially?
10. Will my child be okay?
11. Will people judge us?

All of these questions have answers. To address some of them, you'll need help from an expert like an attorney, accountant, or financial planner. Others we'll handle in this book. Read on...

My Story

I don't talk badly about my ex-husband to anyone, especially not to my son. Just because our marriage didn't work out doesn't mean he's a bad person. He's the father of my son and will always hold a special place in my heart. In fact, my number one concern with writing this book is that I don't want to ever upset him, or my son. I never want them to read what I've written here and feel as if I am saying something bad about either one of them. My ex was in *no way* some horrible person I had to escape. We were just growing in different directions and at different paces. We wanted different things out of life and different lifestyles.

I'll never forget all the wonderful times we shared together. I didn't have my son out of wedlock or force. We both made the decision to have a child together. Sometimes people change and the other partner doesn't change with them. Often, if you marry too young you don't really know what you are looking for; you don't know how to qualify your future partner. You may suffer from regrets, and then feel the need to get things out of your system when you are older. Many people suffer midlife crises. When you have too much responsibility from a young age, it comes back to haunt you later on.

The Catholics have it right by making you take Pre-Cana classes before they will allow you to marry in the Church. My ex-husband and I didn't get married in a church building. Instead, we hired a priest who was willing to marry us off-site. Maybe that was our first mistake. Who knows? At this point, it doesn't matter because I can't undo what's been done. Given all that I've learned, suffice it to say I can't stress the importance of communication in any relationship enough, especially prior to marriage.

When I look back and try to figure out how it went all wrong, I see how I was an active player in it. I guess that is part of being a true adult—admitting your faults, and seeing your weaknesses. You must be honest with yourself as to how your behavior, actions and thoughts led to your divorce. Would I do things differently if I could? Probably. In the moment, I felt as if I was doing everything I could, but in reality, I wasn't doing nearly enough.

I put a lot of the focus on my ex-husband and what I wanted *him* to do and how I wanted *him* to change. Even though I went to counseling on my own for over a year, the therapist was biased and took my side—because she only heard my side. For it to be fair and helpful, it's best for both people to attend at the same time. After a couple of visits together, each person can then attend individually, and occasionally together, based on the therapist's suggestion. Each therapist is not equal. Some are really good, others not so much. You may have to go through several before you both find one that you like and agree on.

My ex-husband moved out of the house when we decided to separate. I honestly felt a big sense of relief. The stress I had been holding onto was released. I had been unhappy for quite some time, so I was ready to move on. Although I cried in the wake of our separation, I cried more while we were still married, living under the same roof. It's far worse to feel lonely when you are lying next to someone than to be alone and lonely.

I will admit I was completely shocked and angry when the Processor came to the house to serve me with divorce papers. I had no idea why this man was banging on my door at 7:00 AM. I was actually so frightened, I called the cops! To my ultimate embarrassment, they found out I was being served.

I know many people would probably lie in bed all day crying and mourning over an experience like this one, but not me. I fed and dressed my son, and we headed over to the gym to get a good workout in. True story! I've always been a survivor. Punch me and I'll get right back up. I am resilient and strong.

Don't get me wrong, however. I was heartbroken that my marriage was ending. Divorce is the death of an intimate relationship. You need to mourn to properly move on. With divorce comes shattered dreams. Somehow, I was able to pull through it. I have a positive outlook on life and believe everything happens for a reason. I do believe I will find true love when I'm fully ready for it.

I remember the exact moment I decided to end my marriage, but I want to preface this section by again mentioning I don't have anything negative to say about my ex-husband. He is not a bad person. He didn't cheat on me (that I know of). He didn't abuse me. There was nothing scandalous about our marriage. In fact, when I was interviewing attorneys, I remember one saying she didn't think I would go through with the divorce since it wasn't for big reasons—to her, at least.

My decision was years in the making. I was unhappy for a long period of time and was really lonely the last few years of my marriage. I would wake up and cry in the middle of the night and my husband never sensed it. I found it so odd that he never did—I always assumed that the person you were married to would feel your pain. I've since learned how to communicate my needs and feelings, which is a difficult thing for so many of us to do.

I spoke to my girlfriends about my situation for years before finally having my *aha* moment, and went to marriage counseling on my own. I finally gave my husband an ultimatum and told him if he didn't go with me I would end our marriage. He reluctantly joined me. When the therapist gave him a specific homework assignment, however, he just could not seem to do what she had asked him to do.

After our first session together, the therapist suggested he go on his own to work on his own issues. He needed to work on himself prior to working on our relationship. I agreed to this plan and understood we would not have immediate results. But he didn't really want to go and said nothing would change—he wouldn't change and our relationship wouldn't change. That was the defining moment for me.

At that time, I didn't know about fixed versus growth mindset. I only knew I didn't like the sounds of what he was saying, and that keeping things the way they were just wouldn't work out for me. I was unhappy for too many years. I figured I was young enough to start all over again. I lost my dad at a young age, and it taught me that life is too short to be unhappy. Tomorrow is not promised to anyone.

As I said, I knew our marriage was not in a good place for a long time. It was especially obvious to me each time we went on vacation. I remember being in Punta Cana and not being happy, thinking to myself how sad it was that we couldn't seem to feel good, even in paradise. I felt the same feelings every time we would go to Florida to visit his family. It was staring me right in the face, the fact that we weren't connecting and enjoying our visits as a couple.

We even went on a final romantic Sandals vacation, just the two of us, with hopes of saving our marriage. That is when I fully realized the extent of our disconnect and lack of communication. It was like walking on eggshells. We had to keep our discussions very neutral to avoid disagreeing. When you are in a relationship, you should be able to fully express yourself.

My parents had an epic love affair and I wanted the same for myself. I wanted that happy family life for my son and I wanted more children. Once I made up my mind about what to do, I felt relief. It was difficult to bring up the topic of my husband moving out, but I knew it was necessary—I saw no point in maintaining the status quo. Once I make my mind up on something, I tend to follow through with it, so when I asked him to move out, I wanted it done pretty quickly.

I can't say I felt sad at that point, because I was unfulfilled for so many years. If anything, the decision to part gave me hope for my future happiness and new beginnings. The unknown was something to look forward to. Of course, I felt guilt regarding my son, for completely changing his world. It's a horrible feeling knowing you are breaking up your own family—you feel completely selfish. A lot of self-doubt and judgment comes into play.

I would tell myself not to be scared. That there is no shame in your choice to create a better life for your family. That you can do it on your own and redefine your image of family. Once you've done that, you will be able to create a better life than you ever imagined. ~Kendra

My son was young at the time, so he didn't completely understand or question what was going on. My ex worked various shifts, so we didn't have a set routine or schedule. He moved an hour away to stay at his friend's house closer to his job. For me, life pretty much went on. I kept up with my usual activities. We had decided to just separate initially, hence my shock at being served. In the long run, however, it was a good thing. Becoming separated got the ball rolling.

What I didn't expect was how incredibly difficult it was going to be to start all over again. I lived in this bubble and had no idea the realities of life. I went from my parents taking care of me to my husband providing for me. I met my husband one year out of college. I didn't really date around much, so I didn't have much experience. I had the same boyfriend all four years of college, and then quickly found a serious relationship with my husband. We were engaged within the year and married the next. It was such a whirlwind and I was so young.

I never really put too much thought into it all. As a result, dating 15 years later proved to be quite a shock! Dating apps, creepy guys, players—that is *not* what I was expecting. I naively thought I would quickly find a guy to replace my husband. Boy, was that bubble popped.

All that said, maybe being a little naive is a good thing sometimes. Perhaps had I known just how hard my life was going to be, I might have stuck it out with my ex. It's like childbirth. You hear stories from other mothers but don't truly know how hard labor can be until you are in it. There is no turning back at that point. Then, once your baby is born, it is all worth it. Divorce is similar. Keep your eye on the prize and know it's all worth it in the end.

> *Never give up. Giving up isn't an option.*

Approach Divorce with Both Eyes Open

Now that I've shared a bit about my personal story, I want to give you some advice. The person you divorce is not the person you married. Don't underestimate what they're capable of doing; please don't go into it being ignorant. I think a lot of women begin the process of divorce still trusting their husbands and say things like, "He'd never do that to me." (Whatever *that* may be in your situation.) I reply, "Girl, I've seen it happen over and over again. Please."

Don't feel guilty about taking care of yourself and your kids financially, doing what you have to do to achieve a fair settlement. Fight for what you deserve, and don't feel guilty about it. You two were married, and fair's fair. What you agree to in your divorce settlement is going to affect you for the rest of your life, so don't give up so easily.

This too shall pass! ~Sherry

Be Cautious About Mediation

People who say, "We're just going to do mediation" make me nervous. Mediation, or a pro se divorce, is when you reach a settlement with no attorneys involved. I've seen so many women lose out that way because they don't know what to fight for, or they are unaware, legally, what they could get in a settlement as the standard in their state. People think, "Oh, mediation will be great, we won't be fighting, it'll be less expensive." It may be less expensive upfront, but you may not get what you deserve in the long run.

Find a Lawyer You Trust

I always tell women, "Please, interview three lawyers." They'll do it for free; there is no charge for a consultation. Go by recommendations from your friends, because not all lawyers are equal. You want someone who is responsive and has a good reputation. During that first consultation, get an idea of what's possible and what's available to you, and what you deserve. Be proactive and not so trusting. If you stayed home and raised the kids, you may feel guilty taking a chunk of the money. But you really shouldn't, because that was your money, together. You just had different roles.

I met with three attorneys for complimentary consultations. They basically all told me the same thing. Looking back, I probably should have gone with a female attorney, one who was more aggressive. At the time, I wanted to avoid the divorce getting ugly, but I feel my attorney was way too complacent. I belong to several single moms' groups, and almost every person complains about their attorney— horrible turnaround times, high expenses, lack of communication, etc.

My divorce was pretty straightforward. We met individually with our attorneys. Then, the four of us had an in-person meeting and the agreement was drawn up. We signed and that was about it. I never stepped foot in court, so I have no idea how that process works, nor do I have any desire to know. I have read too many posts from single moms about court nightmares and games. I chose to not invest my energy into that because what you focus on expands. I choose to focus on peace. Good or bad, I am the type of person who abhors drama. I absolutely hate it when people are upset with me. It makes my heart pound like crazy and my whole body shakes. Maybe it's the hippie in me—who knows? I even joined a moms group called No Drama Mommas, haha. As I am learning and growing, however, I realize the importance and benefits of open communication and honesty, even if it does lead to drama. Hey—I am work in progress, too. I never said I was perfect. I'd be totally lying if I told you that.

One word of caution for those of you in the thick of conflict: keep your affairs private. Don't be stupid and post stuff on social media. It can be held against you. Don't be shady or play games.

Keep your head up, love your babies, and remember, the hardest part will soon be behind you! ~Amanda Marie

Advice from a Family Law Attorney

When you hire an attorney, we understand it's not that you want to ramp up litigation—at all. Attorneys are the ones who make divorce smooth. You don't want to fight. Sure, it's fun for *me* to go to court, but I'll tell you what, it's not fun for my clients. They don't want to do it. So, if you can make agreements and settle things with your attorneys around a table, do it. It will save everybody a lot of money and a lot of animosity. It'll keep your kids from being pawns. When you work with a family law attorney, you'll know that your T's are crossed and your I's are dotted.

Build a Budget

If you have been out of the workforce for some time, the first thing on your To Do list as you begin the separation and divorce process is figuring out if you have access to all of your family's financial information. What can you get your hands on? Because a lot of times, one of the spouses may have been frozen out of financial decisions or were never involved. So, the first thing we have to do when we meet is begin an awakening process.

My client may have no idea how to create a monthly budget—what they would need, what their electrical bill is each month, how much their cell phone costs. It's about getting a handle on what financial information you have access to, and start building a budget and an awareness of what your needs and living expenses are. I'll want to know, what are your fixed expenses? Do you have a mortgage payment? Do you have car loans? Does somebody have student loans out there? In every divorce, you have a finite amount of income. So, we really need to understand the budget.

Gather Financial Statements

Get your hands on your tax returns for the last few years. Gather your financial account statements—checking accounts, savings accounts, investment information (401ks, IRAs, stocks, bonds, whatever)—

before we file for divorce. As soon as the filing happens, it's common for individuals who have been stay-at-home parents to find that the spigot of financial information is shut off. I can ultimately get it even if my client cannot, but it costs more because I have to go through formal discovery processes.

Next, if someone chooses to retain me, we have a meeting in my office and talk through everything: does their spouse know this is coming? If it's not out of the blue, have they talked about what the arrangements are going to be for living, particularly if there are minor children? Have they talked about how they want to deal with placement situations?

Custody and Placement

Courts today, at least here in my state, make a placement schedule for children that maximizes and equalizes the time each parent gets, as long as that is in the best interest of the child. What that means is gone are the days when the wife is automatically getting primary placement of the children. Learning this is very, very difficult for people who have been in medium- to longer-length marriages as stay-at-home parents. It's really hard for them to understand that while they may have been the primary caregiver, when they file for divorce, the roles are going to change. You're not automatically going to continue to be that primary caregiver. Most likely, you're going to have to go out and get a job to support yourself.

Some parents—often mothers—feel violated by this, and can get very defensive. I always say, listen, I agree with you that you've always been there for the kids. This has been your role and it absolutely should be appreciated. That being said, you're taking one household and splitting it into two, so you're each going to be taking up duties that you haven't previously had to do. It is definitely much harder to get moms to realize this than dads. Ultimately, they get it. But sometimes it takes a while. I'm half lawyer, half hairdresser.

Timeframe

The length of the divorce process totally depends on whether you have an agreement in regard to the kids. There are two different tracks a divorce can take. Number one is when two parties have an agreement about placement. From there, we can basically move right into discussing the financials: how we are dividing property. If there is not an agreement, things can take a lot longer. The court will appoint an attorney who acts on behalf of the interests of the children and makes a recommendation to the court regarding custody and placement. The longest divorce case that I've ever had was two years and three months.

If you have a full agreement on everything, it's still a minimum of 120 days before you can get a divorce—but it never happens that fast. It's a scheduling issue with all the courts and attorneys. Six months to a year is more typical.

Mediation

Be very cautious about pro se mediation (this is when you try to negotiate your divorce without hiring attorneys). Half the time the mediator doesn't know what they are doing, and you can end up with a really bad agreement. Then, it is so much more difficult to break that agreement open and start over from the beginning. The case now involves a bunch of presumptions and statutory criteria that wasn't there before. It takes me twice as long to redo everything than it would to do it the right way the first time.

Payment

I work at a big firm, but all the reputable family law attorneys I know require a retainer upfront. My retainers for a divorce, depending on the case, are usually $4,500.00 to $6,500.00. We put that into a trust fund, and I pull out my fees and costs from that fund. I charge at a rate of $245.00/hour and generate monthly statements. There's also a filing fee here of $211.00 that you have to pay to the county. This fee would also come out of the retainer trust fund. Now, a huge problem with family law is that people run out of their retainers and then don't like to pay their lawyers the addition amount owed. One of my downfalls is I'm too nice!

If you meet with several attorneys and one of them does not collect a retainer, that is a huge red flag. It means they are probably not good or established in the family law area. You get what you pay for. My retainer is probably higher than 60% of the attorneys in the area; my hourly rate is very standard.

I tell everyone, "I can marry you in 15 minutes. It's basically free. To divorce you, however, you could be looking at a two-year process, and it could cost you $5,000 to $20,000." So, think it through.

Get a Prenup

If you are contemplating a second marriage, or going into a marriage with some money, get a prenuptial agreement! It will make your divorce so much easier. If you have anything that you'd like to keep at the end of the day, houses, retirement accounts, whatever, sign a prenup. You can get a simple one—you're looking at $2,500 to $3,500 from start to finish.

If you have kids from a first marriage and want to make sure your assets are preserved for those particular children, you need a prenup. Without one, if you die, everything you have is going to your new spouse.

Questions Stay-at-Home Moms May Want to Ask During Initial Attorney Consultations:

1. Are there any tasks I should complete regarding family or personal finances *before* broaching the topic of separating with my husband?
2. I am a stay-at-home mom with no personal income. Will I be okay after a divorce? At what point in this process will I need to begin to work?
3. Should I take steps to ensure family property and accounts are in my name as well as my husband's before filing?
4. Should I get a job before filing for divorce? I've heard that in some states it is better to show little to no income if you were a stay-at-home mom during the majority of the marriage. Is this true?

Thriving Single Moms:

- Practice resiliency, consistency and adaptability.
- Implement good stress management skills.
- Instill independence and limits in their children.
- Have high expectations of themselves and their children (but not to an unrealistic extreme).
- Have a healthy relationship with their child's father.
- Are educated and self-motivated to succeed.
- Actively build a strong bond and relationship with their children.
- Teach their children the value of effort versus results.
- Choose to maintain a positive growth mindset.
- Have routines and structure in the household.
- Build a strong social network and strong faith.
- Practice good communication skills.
- Tend to be givers who volunteer.
- Prioritize quality time as a family.
- Believe in personal development.
- Work to grow their self-confidence.
- Tend to be open-minded, empathic and non-judgmental.
- Are committed to family and success.
- Tend to be financially responsible and frugal.
- Don't take life too seriously and see the humor in situations.
- Practice self-love and self-control.

Chapter 2: Self-Care and Mindset: From Victim to Warrior

*Take care of yourself so you can
take care of your children.*

As single moms, we are always rushing around. We are on call 24/7, with little concern for our personal needs and desires. It seems like there are never enough hours in the day to complete everything that needs to be done. There are days you wish you could clone yourself. Life certainly is not easy for single moms. If you're lucky, you can squeeze in having some sort of an adult social life once things settle down, and possibly even a boyfriend. It's a balancing act. Having free time for ourselves feels like a luxury, yet it is imperative that we make the space for kid-free time. You'll hear me echo this sentiment again and again in this chapter.

We face the challenge of work, being a mom, and maintaining a personal life. Relaxing isn't a part of our vocabulary and neither is boredom. I wish I could remember a time when I was bored! Sleep and relaxation are valuable luxuries that I took for granted when they were abundant. Those moments are long gone, and the feeling nearly forgotten. It is easy to constantly feel stressed out and anxious. There is very little down time, which is why self-care is so essential.

On the roughest days, please remember:

- You are a badass mom.
- You are not broken.
- Be patient with yourself.
- Do what you have to do.

I take time for myself, and I try to do it without guilt. Let me repeat that: *I choose self-care without guilt.* Stress makes you feel as if you have aged tremendously. Stress also makes it harder for you to lose weight and can cause disease. It's not something you should ignore, yet we put our children's needs before our own. We give, give, and give. Full disclosure: I'm *still* trying to learn how to say no to people.

Moms don't blink an eye when it comes to taking care of others, but we struggle to take time out for ourselves. We need to rejuvenate and relax. The saying "You can't pour from an empty cup" is true. I know it's difficult to do, but we must put our pride and guilt aside, and ask for assistance when we need it. Your true friends and family will want to help you, so ask for help without guilt and accept it without guilt!

Self-care helps you stay in control of your emotions and reactions to life's stressors, and it doesn't have to be expensive. Watching a sunset or sunrise is free and something you can do daily. Give someone you love a hug. Hugging has numerous benefits, including boosting your immunity.

Make time for self-care—block it into your schedule. For the moms with newborns, the laundry, dishes and chores can wait. That is my number one rule. You are in survival mode in the beginning and you must take care of yourself so you can take care of the baby.

Express Yourself

Call your girlfriends when you need to vent. I highly recommend having a good friend you can talk with regularly. It is healthy to get things off of your chest, and to speak to a trusted friend who can validate your feelings and struggles. Sometimes just being heard on those hard days can be so rejuvenating.

Keep a journal and write down how you are feeling. Putting pen to paper can be very powerful and release lots of negative energy. Write a letter to a friend telling them how much you appreciate them. Very rarely do people receive handwritten letters from loved ones. Do an ugly cry whenever you need to—it is so cleansing for the soul. Don't compare yourself to other moms. Parents, children and situations are unique.

More Quick Ideas for Soothing Self-Care

- Without overdoing it, have that glass of wine when you need to relax.
- Epsom salt baths with a good novel can help you escape from reality for a little bit. Join a book club so you will be more likely to take the time to read for pleasure.
- Light some candles and enjoy some quiet time alone.
- Indulge in dark chocolate when you need something sweet—a little goes a long way. If you enjoy baking, try a new recipe.
- Fifteen-minute chair massages at the mall are super convenient and affordable.
- Listening to music of any genre can be so uplifting, depending on the mood you are in and the mood you want to experience.
- Have herbal tea at night before bed.
- Diffuse lavender oil in your bedroom at bedtime.
- Do a home facial and a mani/pedi.
- Look through old photo books and letters.
- It may seem like you don't have any down time, but volunteering and helping those in need shifts the focus off your life for a while and can help you appreciate what you have.
- Do a five-minute meditation and gratitude practice before bed.
- Try stating positive affirmations daily (turn to the end of this chapter for some ideas) and listen to uplifting audiobooks or podcasts. You can download many apps right onto your mobile phone.

When You Need to Reset

I used to find myself being tired and cranky all the time, and my patience level was low. I realized the importance of making myself a priority. (Or, at the very least, adding myself to the list!) Now, I make the time to relax and do fun, adult things. I learned that once I start feeling stressed out, I need to take a break from work and chores and do something enjoyable. I have adapted the mentality that I can live without my house being in perfect condition. It is more important that I make time for my son. Cherish your loved ones, learn to let go and release the urge to control every single thing or have perfection in all areas of your life.

Go outside and soak up nature; this is so soothing to the soul. If you are super stressed out, go into a different room or go outside. Changing your environment can do wonders for you. Also, get your body moving, because motion changes emotion. Do 30 seconds of jumping jacks and see how quickly your mood can shift. I often tell my clients to be "naughty." Let that inner child come out and do something just for the fun of it. Prank call a friend; wear a wig for a day. Let your inner creative self emerge. Draw, paint, enjoy adult coloring books.

Reflections from a Single Mom of Twins

To the mother who is newly single or doing it alone from the get-go: You were given this challenge because you are one of the select few who are strong enough to handle it. It's not easy, nothing ever is, but when you look back years from now, you won't be remembering all of the hard times. You'll be reminiscing on those special moments of seeing your child walk, or hearing them say "momma" for the first time, or taking their first step into kindergarten. You are going to look back and wonder why you worried so much and why you didn't enjoy it more.

Your life is going to be messy, in every sense of the word, but you have to remind yourself that you are amazing and you can do this. Only women have the ability to create life, the most powerful gift there is, and if we can do that, we can do just about anything. So, when you're sad or feel like giving up, take a deep breath, look into your child's eyes, and you will find your strength.

I went into my pregnancy with the attitude of, "There's no going back." I made the decision to be a mom and I stand by it 100%. When you have a child, it's no longer about your needs but about theirs. You change your mindset to what will benefit their life and grow upon that. I didn't have a lot when I had my twins, and I still don't. It was really tough to try and stay positive when it seemed there was always something around the corner that was going to put me further in the hole. I've had my down moments, but when I look at my two beautiful kids, I remember why I'm enduring it. The negativity will always try and get to you, but you have to keep fighting to stay positive. If you can't do it for yourself, do it for your children. They deserve a happy mother; they feel what you are going through.

I always found loading up the kids in the car and driving somewhere new to be super refreshing. It gave me something to look forward to instead of our daily routines. It got me out of my head, which allowed time to remind myself to enjoy my journey.

I think self-care is more about a healthy mind rather than a spa day or shopping trip. It's about remembering who you are and where you want to be. Self-reflecting is so vital for mothers. I hear, so often, that mothers feel like they are losing themselves with full days of mom duties that turn into years. Don't let yourself get to that point; you need to still have "you time" in the midst of all the chaos. Always find time to recharge and restart.

Now that my children are two years old, I think the hardest part of my day is making dinner after a full day at work. It leads to cleaning, bath time, fighting for bedtime, and when you think you finally have a second to yourself, you have to study. While it is exhausting, I find it to be more frustrating because there's never enough hours in a day when you become a mother. My list of "To Do's" continuously grows longer and I'm constantly trying to grasp any amount of time I can. ~Berkley

Self-Love

Tell your reflection you love yourself. Say it at the mirror each day until you fully believe it. Unfollow people on social media if they are too negative, political or judgmental. It's so incredibly freeing. You will be a positive role model for your children when you show them what self-love and self-care is. Wouldn't it be great to teach our young daughters the very same thing most grown women find challenging?

Take time to learn something new every day. Take an online course. Watch a comedy, go to a comedy show. Laughter can be the best medicine! Smile at people and see how they react. Sit in the sun for 10 minutes and feel the warmth on your face. Be gentle on yourself. Practice positive self-talk. Release the old stories you tell yourself.

Let go of guilt, shame and embarrassment. Forgive others and move on.

Be sure to get adequate sleep and rest. Insufficient sleep can lead to serious health issues like diabetes, heart disease, depression, and accidents. Again, don't allow your own health to take a back seat. You won't be doing anyone any favors if you get sick. Your family deserves to receive the best version of you, the A-version. That will not be possible unless you take care of yourself, emotionally and physically.

Take the help when it is offered. Hire a babysitter and spend time/money on yourself, without feeling bad. Enjoy a glass of wine, no one will judge. ~Kristini

Boundaries and Me Time

Women need to learn how to ask for what they need from family members and friends, and how to create healthy boundaries. If we don't respect ourselves, how can we expect others to respect us? Create healthy boundaries for yourself.

I know how busy your life is, and I understand the overwhelming stress you feel constantly. A few years ago, I moved to a state where I have no family to help me. However, I still make sure I get sleep and exercise. I make my health a priority and live by my calendar. I schedule my workout sessions and other activities so I can keep track of it all and stay organized.

Remember, you aren't only a mom but an individual—don't lose yourself in motherhood. I never understood those moms who said they can't bear to be away from their kids. Really? Personally, I need a break for my sanity. If you spend too much time with anyone, they will eventually get annoying. I need my girlfriend time. Make sure you have fun and enjoy life.

Your faith and community can also be a great avenue for you as you heal from your divorce. Talking to a mental health specialist can help if you feel like you are drowning or depressed. Our children need us to be mentally strong and healthy to be the best parents we can be. Failing to take care of yourself can lead to resentment in the long-term, which is not good for anyone.

The Martyr Trap

One thing I want to touch upon is the subject of martyrdom. Many moms fall into this trap and may be proud of themselves for always putting others first. The reality is, however, that you can be a better mom if you make yourself a priority. Your worth and meaning does not come solely from how much you give to others. Your family will still love and recognize your efforts. Actually, they will respect and appreciate you *more* in the long run if you choose to prioritize self-care. There is no upside to constant self-sacrifice. On the contrary, there is a steep price to pay when you are constantly under stress. Your body is overwhelmed and in fight or flight mode. This, in turn, lowers your immune system's ability to function.

As single moms, our responsibilities are not going anywhere, so we must learn how to handle stress and find balance. We cannot be all things for all people at all times. There is only one you and only 24 hours in day. Learn to say no and remove activities and events that don't truly serve you.

In the spring, my aging mom moved to Florida to live with me. All of a sudden, I had so much more on my already-filled plate. I was stressed beyond belief and didn't even realize it. I started noticing my hair falling out. That was not normal for me. I waited a few months and then went to my General Physician for my yearly blood work. Everything came back fine. He even did extra testing at my request. I was stumped. It winds up it was all due to stress!

After talking to other female friends, I learned they had experienced the same thing. It truly is amazing, and scary, how stress can affect you. It all goes back to that mind/body connection. Stress literally is a killer. You absolutely *must learn* how to handle it. Our harried lifestyle and obligations are a fact of life, so we must create coping skills and take care of ourselves.

Long term stress causes inflammation in your body. It can also cause psychological issues such as depression and anxiety. It is truly an epidemic in our society right now and

I think this is why so many people self-medicate with alcohol, pills and drugs.

Your mental health plays a critical role in your parenting ability. This is a very important topic and the area I focus on for my coaching clients.

It's okay to feel scared and nervous. It's okay to feel anxious. It's okay to feel overwhelmed and like you might fail or, hell, maybe feel like you already did fail. It's okay to feel alone. But know you WILL get through.

Not because you have to, which you do, for the sake of your little one(s). Not because you want to, which I am sure you do. Not because someone else will carry you, which they will, when you're ready to throw in the towel. But because you're a mom. And that's what we do. We get through it and we do the best we possibly can to make sure ourselves and our little ones are taken care of. Because we know we don't have a choice. We know the true meaning of sacrifice. Moms make it happen. We are superheroes!

Make time for yourself. Whether it be daily or weekly or monthly. Just plan it into your schedule. The gym, your nails, a run, a walk, a shop, a DATE (yes, learn to date again). Find your people, your village. Those who will watch your little so that you can take care of you, too! ~Amy

Setting Priorities

As a society, we must learn to stop being so busy and just *be*. Figure out what your priorities are and allot time for them. Design the life that you want and deserve. Let go of other obligations that are sapping your time and energy.

We are always at different seasons of our lives. Some seasons we will have more time to volunteer, other times we won't. That is okay. You are the CEO of your life. Cut out people who bring you down or waste your time. At the end of the day, you must First Love Yourself, FLY. We always win the game we play and believe the story we tell ourselves. If you say you are too busy to take care of yourself, then you will be too busy—and will most likely continue to be. Are you a victim or are you in control of your life?

Getting divorced is a hard decision. It takes years of unhappiness to get to that point. Even though being divorced can be difficult, life is too short to be in an unhappy relationship. Sometimes parting ways is the best thing for everyone involved, even if it doesn't seem like it at the time. As I mentioned in the previous chapter, I'm much happier in many ways now that I'm not married. The transition from having a partner to being on your own is tough, however, and the challenge of getting through it to better days shouldn't be underestimated. The good news is it does get easier with time.

Nutrition

Stress management is critical and a major needle-mover in one's health. Divorce is one of the most stressful things someone can go through, but proper nutrition helps so much. Ask your friends to do a food train when you're having a rough week so you don't have to worry about cooking. Stay hydrated and make time to eat. Listen to your body—it's is your greatest lab experiment. Play around. There is no one right diet for everyone.

Treating yourself to eating out at a favorite restaurant during a particularly busy week can be a good option. Also, there are now options to have healthy meals delivered to you through services such as Hello Fresh and Blue Apron. Some provide the ingredients while others deliver the food fully prepared—so no prep work necessary!

You need your health and energy to get through the difficulties of divorce and be a good parent, so be aware of simple versus complex carbohydrates and try to choose complex options when you can—whole wheat, vegetables and whole fruits instead of juices. These are some areas I go further into depth with my coaching clients—to help them lose weight, gain energy, and feel good. These changes trickle through other aspects of their lives, such as improved relationships with family members and more confidence to achieve goals. Make the effort to have balanced blood sugar and avoid the ups and downs of the sugar roller coaster ride—it causes enormous biological and chemical stress on the body, destroying good health. Eating excess added sugar in any form regularly will cause weight gain, low energy, poor health and disease.

Names for sugar on food labels:

- Sucrose, fructose or lactose
- High-fructose corn syrup
- Barley malt
- Beet sugar or grape sugar
- Honey or molasses
- Brown sugar
- Buttered syrup
- Cane juice crystals or dehydrated cane juice
- Caramel
- Carob syrup
- Corn syrup solids
- Date sugar
- Dextran or dextrose
- Diastase
- Ethyle maltol
- Fruit juice concentrate
- Glucose or glucose solids
- Malt syrup
- Maltodextrin
- Maltose
- Mannitol
- Raw sugar
- Sorbitol
- Sorghum syrup
- Sucrose
- Xylitol

With good nutrition comes proper hydration. Make sure you are drinking enough water. The human body is 55%-60% water. The benefits of adequate water consumption are so numerous:

- Increases energy and brain power
- Promotes healthy weight and weight loss
- Detoxes your body
- Improves complexion
- Maintains regularity
- Boosts immune system
- Prevents headaches
- Prevents cramps and sprains
- Helps regulate your body temp
- Prevents backaches
- Improves heart health
- Prevents bad breath
- Helps with hangovers
- Improves your mood

Drink between 64 ounces and 67% of your body weight. For example, if your body weight is 150 pounds, drink anywhere between 64 ounces and 100 ounces of water per day. The amount of water you should drink also depends on your activity level, caffeine intake, alcohol consumption and the air temperature.

When you are drinking adequate water, your urine will be on the light side. Dark urine is an indication of dehydration. It is normal to feel the urge to hit the bathroom every few hours. Eventually, your body will adjust.

Tips and tricks to increase your water consumption:

- Drink two glasses upon waking in the morning.
- Always keep a water bottle with you.
- Keep water glasses throughout your house and office space.
- Drink prior to, during, and post workout.
- Use a water app as a reminder to drink more water.
- Use a fancy glass.
- Add fruit or herbs (lemon, lime, cucumber, orange, mint leaves) to your water to increase the flavor. Add Emergen-C to your water. Remember, herbal tea counts!

Our food is not just nourishment for the body, it's also nourishment for the soul. That's why so many people have issues with emotional eating—they are trying to fill a void in their lives. If this sounds familiar to you, the first step is to be conscious that emotional eating might be something you're doing, then find other ways to address and honor your emotions.

It can helpful to get to the why. What I mean by this is asking questions such as, "What is this sweetness, this flavor, giving me?" Most people crave sweets because they're craving more happiness in their lives.

As a coach, my job is to help my clients identify what they're lacking, and find a healthier substitution than sweets for filling the void. A lot of people come to me for weight loss, but when you start digging, there's usually a much deeper story than just someone's desire to lose weight.

So, that's how I approach things. I'm not interested in telling someone to cut calories. I'm more holistic, and I want to see what's going on in their lives. I also want people to count chemicals, not calories. You should be way more worried about the crap that's in your food than calories. If you just eat real food in moderation, you're automatically going to lose weight. Anything that's "no fat" or "low fat" is chemical warfare. You should be more scared of that than of calories.

My philosophy on nutrition and overall health in general is so many people are a slave to numbers on a scale, and that's *so* not healthy. Eat meals together as a family and try to make them last at least twenty minutes. In this day and age, twenty minutes feels long. When you actually put the timer on, you realize most people aren't sitting down for twenty minutes. They're scarfing down their meals.

Savor your food. Drink between bites. Put your fork down. What I do with my son is some gratitude practices while we are eating. Talk about what you're grateful for. It's an ideal time for the family to connect and appreciate everything that they *do* have in their lives right now, versus looking at the negatives. Meal time is a great time to talk about the highs and lows of the day, as in, "What was your favorite part of the day?" "What happened at school?"

Ensuring Your Kids Eat Healthfully

Depending on their ages, include kids in food shopping and meal preparation. This helps them be more open to trying new things, to eating vegetables. If it's possible, help them grow their own small garden, just so they can start learning real food is grown in soil. It helps to see herbs grow, and see food as an energy source. Because that's what it is, it's meant to nourish your body.

So many people skip meals when they're trying to lose weight, or when they're too busy. I don't recommend this. When you're going through a divorce, you definitely need energy to get you through. Furthermore, when you skip a meal your body goes into starvation mode because it doesn't know when it's getting its next meal. This actually makes your body hold onto fat, making it more difficult to lose weight. It slows down your metabolism. Also, you're being a model for your children. If you're not taking care of yourself and eating properly, then they're going to follow that example. They're going to do what you do, not what you say.

It can help to do little tricks with food preparation, particularly for those mothers who have picky eaters. I used to sneak foods into meals, and my son had no idea. I took pureed sweet potatoes, for example, and put them into pancakes. Pumpkin puree in tomato sauce, or blueberries into brownie batter—simple little things that add a nutrient punch. Smoothies can be a good option.

More Ideas for Helping Your Kids Get Their Veggies...Without Even Knowing It

- Add minced broccoli or cauliflower to omelets.
- Put grated zucchini or carrots into baked muffins.
- Add blended pumpkin or butternut squash to pancakes and waffles.
- Put some greens into fruit smoothies—fresh spinach blends up very nicely.
- Add dark chocolate to smoothies to hide the greens.
- Sprinkle herbs on top of dishes. This is super healthy and a great way to help your kids appreciate a wider variety of flavors!
- Make homemade mac 'n cheese with peas in it.
- Sneak veggies into casseroles.
- Sneak veggies into grilled cheese sandwiches—tomatoes are tasty!
- Add corn and other veggies like green or red pepper to cheese quesadillas.
- Add carrot puree to ground beef for burgers or meatballs.
- Put pureed carrots into tomato sauce.
- Bake kale chips in your oven instead of regular fries.
- Throw veggies into soups.
- Add pureed spinach into brownies.
- Add carrots or squash to chocolate cake. Chocolate hides a lot of flavors!
- Put sweet potato puree in your chocolate chip cookie batter.

Be sure to watch the consistency of the food so kids don't realize what you are trying to do. I prefer using pureed fruits and veggies. Textures are huge for kids, and some adults too!

Fitness: Break it Down and Make the Time

I've been a personal trainer for over a dozen years, and I'm also an aerobics instructor. I'm certified in everything from prenatal to children, all the way up to seniors. I do it all: water aerobics, step, yoga, spin, Zumba, kickboxing, Pilates. I have a lot of experience with movement; fitness is my forte.

If you're just starting out, break it down. I believe in baby steps, starting with small increments of physical activity. People who have the biggest changes to make generally can only handle small changes at once, but that's okay—small hinges swing big doors. Think of an airplane. If you change your course by one degree, you are landing in a totally different destination. It's the same thing with good self-care habits and fitness. Start with something that's manageable. One thing at a time, don't go crazy. If you get too sore at the beginning, you're going to stop altogether.

If you can exercise 15 minutes a day, that's great. Or even twice a day. Walk. Get out in the fresh air, or even on a treadmill. Fifteen minutes at once is better than nothing. Do it during commercial breaks or while you're watching TV. Involve the kids. I used to walk with my son in the stroller all the time, or jog next to him when he was riding on his bike. No excuses. I wore him in a baby carrier on my stationary bike, sweating to death. You can exercise when your children are taking a nap, or when they're at school or daycare. It's really important to keep that fitness element in your life. For me, exercise is my therapy, my mental release. Physical movement releases endorphins, the feel-good hormone. Exercise gives me the energy I need to make it through my busy mom life. I sleep better at night. Especially when you're going through a tough time, sleep is so critical. Proper nutrition and fitness will help you get through it.

Moms have a lot of guilt when it comes to their babies and their kids in general. But there's nothing wrong with setting aside the time to go to the gym. In my case, I said, "This is the one thing I'm still going to do for myself. I'm not going to let that go." My son used to scream at the gym's nursery. But they would say, "It's okay, just go, he'll calm down in a few minutes." It was so hard to do, but they were right. He would calm down. The more I brought him, the more he got used to it. Until there were no more tears.

You have to do this for yourself. I have so many friends who say, "Oh, I can't do that to my kid, I feel too selfish." But you're really not being selfish when you take care of yourself. When you're in a better place, physically, mentally, emotionally, you're a much better parent.

There are so many fitness options today. You can do Stroller Strides, water aerobics, step, yoga, spin, Zumba, Pilates; many gyms have nurseries. You can work out from home with YouTube. There's no excuse, even financially. Go on Pinterest. It has tons of workouts. There is so much free information out there. There are hundreds of fitness apps you can download right onto your phone. Use your own body weight, you don't need fancy equipment. If you work, walk on your lunch break.

If it's something you really want, you're going to make it happen. Too many people make excuses because fitness is not their priority. They say they want it, but *saying* you want it is not enough.

Do something that you love, because if it's not enjoyable you're not going to stick with it. There are so many different modalities of fitness, and I believe more in movement versus exercise. It's a mindset: "I can handle movement." Maybe take a dance class, or dance with your friends. It doesn't have to be CrossFit. Make it enjoyable. Try different things, and see what works for you, see what you're going to stick with.

My Coaching Journey

As I said previously, I have been a Personal Trainer for over a decade. Initially, I worked in various gyms. Then I decided to take control of my schedule and level of pay and ventured off to in-home Personal Training. I absolutely love it. It allows me the freedom and flexibility I desire and need as a single mom. Since I see my clients on a recurring basis in an intimate setting, they tend to open up to me and ask for advice and tips. It was the perfect segue into Health & Life Coaching. I was basically already doing this kind of coaching for my clients, so eventually it was time to study and get certified.

While studying, I learned the reason many clients don't find true health success with just the physical aspect of training: You need the nutrition piece in place and proper mindset in all aspects of wellness to be truly successful in your health and fitness goals. There is something to be said about the mind, body, soul connection. Health is so much more than just the physical side of it—in fact, there are seven dimensions of wellness. Each plays a contributing role in your overall health. Finding balance is imperative for true health.

Even with nutrition, it is not just about the foods that you eat, but how you eat, your mindset and the soul nourishment. Controlling blood sugar and stress are two major needle movers that I teach my coaching and training clients. I could write an entire book on these two subjects alone.

The Seven Dimensions of Wellness

- **Physical:** The ability to get through your daily activities without fatigue or physical stress. This encompasses taking care of your physical body by making informed and responsible decisions about your health. Healthy behaviors include adequate exercise, proper nutrition, and abstaining from harmful habits such as drug and alcohol abuse. You can be very proactive in this area, which will allow you to have a lot of control over your health.

- **Emotional:** Your emotional state is always changing. Being emotionally well means being able to feel and express human emotions, including the ability to love and be loved. Emotional wellness includes being optimistic, practicing self-love, and enjoying positive self-esteem. Having the ability to understand ourselves and cope with life's challenges is an important part of emotional wellness.

- **Intellectual:** This aspect of wellness includes exercising and stimulating your mind—continually learning and practicing self-improvement. It includes being open to new ideas and experiences.

- **Social:** This dimension of wellness refers to one's ability to respectfully interact and relate with others and self. You are able to develop and maintain positive, meaningful relationship with peers. Being social gives you a sense of belonging, which is a basic human need.

- **Spiritual:** Your spirituality gives you a set of guiding beliefs and values that provide you direction in life. It can encompass faith, hope, honesty, forgiveness and compassion to give your life meaning and purpose. Spiritual wellness gives you something bigger than yourself to believe in and helps you in living life to the fullest. Having peace and harmony in your life is an aspect of spiritual wellness.

- **Environmental:** Environmental wellness brings your awareness to our earth and planet. When we have a strong sense of environmental wellness, we try to live in a manner that respects our earth and minimizes its harm by preserving resources. This dimension of wellness involves making a positive impact on the quality of our homes, communities and planet.

- **Occupational:** Occupational wellness involves making use of your gifts and skills to enrich your life and those around you. It means having satisfaction with your career. It is the ability to get personal fulfillment from our jobs while still maintaining balance in our lives.

Handling Injuries

If you're increasing your level of physical activity, you may eventually have to deal with an injury. I always tell my clients, first and foremost, to listen to their bodies. If a particular exercise doesn't feel right, don't do it. There are plenty of ways to modify the movement or just choose something else. It is *never* worth causing injury or further harm. When your body is in pain, it is a signal for you to stop. Your body has infinite wisdom, listen to it.

Suffering an injury always feels like a setback, especially to fitness fanatics who work out regularly. Not only is it a physical setback, it is also a mental one. The mental impact of removing fitness from your routine is almost immediate. If you must take a break from working out for a few days, it is not the end of the world. It is good to allow your body to rest and recuperate so you can come back stronger.

If you suffer a more serious injury, take advantage of your time off to connect with a physical therapist and others who have had the same experience. They may be able to give you some pointers for healing and eventually getting back into your routine. Perhaps they can suggest another form of fitness that won't worsen your current condition. Walking, swimming, cycling and yoga are great modalities that are gentle on your body. If one body part or joint is immobilized, there are usually alternatives for working around it. Try to maintain the right attitude and be flexible with your options. Doing a short circuit with high repetitions, low weight and short rest periods can serve as a cardio workout.

Remember that you can't build strength on top of an injury.
Do not ignore any pain you may be feeling; pain is a
warning sign. Utilize your time off to cook healthy meals
and work on your mental strength through meditation and
mindset.

I am not a fan of extreme fitness. Many people will be
paying for pushing their bodies too hard when they are
older. Always listen to your doctor and get their approval
before commencing any exercise program. You must
proceed with caution; I recommend starting out gradually.
Always start with a warm up by doing dynamic movements.
Try to vary your workouts to prevent overworking the same
muscles. Injuries usually heal faster if you were in shape
prior to the injury occurring. End with a cool down and be
sure to stretch out your muscles to help prevent soreness.

Spirituality

I have strong faith in God. I was raised a strict Catholic,
which in my case meant you didn't miss church unless you
were dying. I even had to go on my birthday because it was
a religious holiday. Can you imagine how much fun that
was as a kid? I went to a Jesuit University and was a
Eucharistic Minister. All that said, don't go thinking I was a
goody two-shoes! Believe me, I have partied in my day. But
seriously, my faith has given me so much strength. I no
longer go to church every week, but I do try to go for my
son, especially since he has been in religious education the
last few years.

Being raised Catholic, I know the church does not believe in divorce. However, I don't believe God would want people to suffer and remain in miserable marriages. Sometimes you just marry the wrong person. Sometimes you can both make an effort to help your relationship work but you just can't make it happen.

As I get older, I am becoming more spiritual versus religious. I don't believe everything the Church preaches; I most certainly have an issue with all the priest abuse. Being kind to others and being a good person seems more important to me than following outdated rules created by men. I'm a very positive person, and I see the good in every situation. I would not allow any religious organization to dictate my life or have me feel guilty about making choices that I believe are best for me. My relationship with God is private and should be of no one else's concern. I do not need to be judged by another human being for my actions or the life I choose to live. It is sad that many people live a life to please or impress others instead of living how they really want to. I even know people who are gay but won't come out to their families if they are a certain religion or nationality.

As you explore your spiritual side, I think it's natural to start questioning what you were brought up with. Does it really resonate with you? Do you agree with what they're preaching when you are sitting there in a service? I didn't agree with everything that the Catholic Church told me, so I started checking out non-denominational services and Lutheran services with my friends. I was always willing to see what was out there, and what was resonating with me. My ex wasn't very religious, so it wasn't something that we did together.

I found this non-denominational church in my town, and love the community feeling. The opening message each week is they welcome everyone, regardless of their sexuality or anything else. I really like that. For me, if God is perfect, then everyone He's creating is perfect. So how can someone who is gay be wrong?

I raise my son Catholic because I want him to have the traditions, and I think it's important for kids to have something in their life, whether it's religion or spirituality. They can then make their own decision about it when they're older. I do bring him to different churches. I tend to connect more with upbeat, positive services.

There are so many different types of churches or spiritual practices to try on. Just find something that speaks to you, that resonates with your soul. Look for a place that makes you feel aligned, as in, "That message was directly for me. That was exactly what I needed today and this week." *That's* when you know you've found your place, when you're with likeminded people who are going to support you and feel the same way.

> *My advice is that you're stronger than you think you are. Lay at the cross, pray, and don't be afraid to ask for help. Let the people who want to help, help. ~Jennifer*

Personal Spirituality

Faith will get you through the hard times. It doesn't have to be a religion or a church. I'm a huge believer in meditation; that's been really good for me. It's something you can start five minutes a day, and makes such a difference. I recommend meditating in the morning, first thing when you get up. An early morning meditation session just sets the tone and your intention for the day. It's also good for when you're stressed out with your kids. Take five minutes, put yourself in a time out. It's amazing how it can just change everything. Motion also changes your feelings—jog in place, or step outside when you need a reset.

When it comes to your spirituality, you have to find what works for you; you can't be influenced by family or friends. I have some friends who are very religious. They don't believe in divorce. People can be really judgmental about it, and even say things such as, "Oh, you're splitting up your family. I could never do that to my kids." I still get this from some individuals, and it hurts.

Spirituality is a very personal and very individualized thing that you can call on at any moment. A lot of your thoughts and beliefs and how you view the world is based on your upbringing. So, if you begin to question it, I think that brings up a lot of guilt for people, which is such a shame. Live your own truth.

No matter how hard things get, take time for you and keep your faith in God. Ask Him for strength; he will see you through! ~Julie

Volunteering and Giving

I am a huge believer in volunteering. I have always volunteered at my son's school in some capacity, whether being a member of the PTA, having a PTA position, being the Class Mom, or volunteering for events and trips. I think it's so important to play an active role in your child's school life in some capacity. Of course, not everyone's work schedule allows for this, but if you are able to help out, it's a great thing.

I love having my son volunteer alongside me. We trained our dog through the local humane society to become a pet therapy dog. Then, we brought her to the local senior citizen homes to visit and cheer them up. Throughout my son's life, I have always had him donate his old toys and clothes to the poor and less fortunate. It is a beautiful thing to teach your child about giving. One of my favorite books is "The Go-Giver" by Bob Burg; one of my all-time favorite quotes is "Service to others is the rent you pay for your room here on earth," attributed to the amazing Muhammad Ali. I've brought my son to beach clean-ups so he can appreciate the significance of maintaining our natural environment. We use stainless steel straws to help protect the earth from too much plastic pollution. We recycle at home and pick up trash in public.

My parents made me volunteer before I was the legal age to start working. I have given away many babysitting sessions so parents can have a break and enjoy themselves. My first volunteer assignment was at the nursery school I attended. I loved that "job." Since then, I have done much work with children. There is just something about the innocence of small kids; I love their energy and positivity—how they notice the little things in life. It is great how children just live in the present moment; adults can learn a lot from children.

Giving helps you focus on someone else and often helps you heal in the process. We are put on this earth to be loving and spread kindness. Give with no expectation of reciprocity. Give not for the fame. My spirituality calls me to be a good person and to help others. Give when you can; it doesn't have to be monetary. Your time is sometimes the best gift you can give someone. Even just listening to someone in need can be a powerful gift beyond measure. Making others feel good about themselves is a wonderful gift to give and costs nothing. Thinking and speaking well of others is a great gift to them as well.

Giving makes our hearts stronger, and in turn, it makes *us* stronger. Another part of giving is being open to receiving. You are giving the giver a gift by receiving. It makes them feel good. Never feel guilty for receiving when you are in need.

Teach the Art of Giving to Your Child

I teach my son the value of paying it forward. On occasion, I will pay for the person behind me in the drive thru at Dunkin Donuts or Starbucks. It's not a huge gesture, but it can brighten someone's day and maybe inspire them to pass it forward. Can you just imagine how our world would be if everyone took the time to do this? Now that my son is getting older, we will also have more volunteering opportunities present themselves as many places require volunteers to be a certain age for liability reasons.

I grew up in New York, and my son spent the first eight years of his life there. We would sometimes go into the city, and I would give him money to hand to the homeless. Any little thing you can do makes a difference in other's lives. We donate to our church, too. I still remember, to this day, giving all my spare change to the collection basket as a child. I think that is when it dawned on me, the importance of giving. I want to instill certain traits, ethics, morals and values in my son. His education, health and happiness are a priority, followed by being a good person and helping others. I remind my son to welcome the new kid at school. He knows the importance of standing up for others and defending them.

Growth Through Compassion

To me, life is about having compassion and empathy for others. I want to make a difference in this world by helping others, so my long-term goal is to be a philanthropist. I want to leave behind a loving legacy. God gave me certain gifts and it is up to me to share them. I was placed on this Earth for a reason. I believe we can accomplish more by helping one another and working together than we can alone. We must act like a community to serve others in a bigger capacity.

Last year, I was there as my best friend's mom was passing away from cancer, a brain tumor. It was a few of the hardest weeks of my life, aside from when my own father passed away. Sleeping in the hospital, being in the Hospice home. It was so incredibly difficult to watch, but I knew they needed me. God called on me to be there for them. That is what life is all about: Being there for one another. It's not just about the fun and easy times. You show your true colors in times of need. My dad had cancer and Scleroderma, which is a chronic connective tissue disease affecting the autoimmune system. His organs hardened, and he died a horrible death. I found strength in God to get me through it, and all my close friends were there for me. Some of my college friends even missed spring exams to be at my dad's funeral. What goes around comes around. When you help others and are a good friend, it comes back to you.

I love being the person my loved ones know they can rely on. I'm not just a good-time friend. I show up early at parties, help set up, and stay to clean. That is what I stand for and hope to pass along to my son.

Be generous with your time and love. People have helped you along the way, and giving helps pay them back. How can you expect God to be generous to you if you are not generous to others?

More Giving Ideas

- Do a food train for someone who is sick or has a new child.
- Do favors when you can. I often have my son's friends here and have them sleepover to give their parents a break. It doesn't take much to help others. It doesn't need to be grand.
- Forgiving others is also a gift of giving.

Emotions and Grief in the Wake of Divorce

Grieving is a roller coaster. You'll have a lot of doubt—did I make the right decision? The guilt can wear you out. You'll second guess yourself, especially when you have kids. You'll wonder if you did the right thing. The first year was definitely the hardest for me, but part of it was just what I put on myself. I can be a very private person, and I was so embarrassed. Only my closest friends knew what was going on. I didn't tell people for the entire first year. Not on social media, not in person, I just kind of stayed in my shell. Then eventually, people started figuring it out.

Get yourself a good support system. My mom was so great, and I'm so blessed to have many amazing friends who were really there for me during my divorce. Don't isolate yourself. That's the worst thing you can do. My friends would take me out if I needed it, just to have a drink, or talk on the phone to get my mind off of things. You need someone who will listen to you and not judge, or even give advice necessarily. Just someone there by your side.

Let go of that judgment and that embarrassment you're putting on yourself. After I got past it, I realized, "Oh my God, there's this whole world of single people out here!" I had never been in that world; my world was married couples with families. Once I went back out there, I realized, "Oh, people who are remarried now were divorced before." I had no idea, I had always just assumed they were on their first marriage. There are so many people in the same position as you—or people who previously were. You're not alone. Don't feel ashamed.

I have girlfriends who are miserable right now in their marriages. They all have kids, and they just can't see or imagine themselves surviving on their own, especially financially. That's probably the biggest thing, particularly for a stay-at-home mom, which I was. There are so many people who are in this boat, and they don't believe in themselves, that they could make it work. They get caught up in the logistics of it, the questions of, "Who would pick up the kids from school?" and "What about their extracurriculars?"

To that I say, it all works out when you are forced to make it work out. Honestly, I had to drop some sports and things for my son because I couldn't afford them, but it was a good thing. Everything in our lives has slowed down.

This society is crazy—kids have to be in five different things; there's no downtime. It's almost as if there's a competition between moms on who has the busiest kids, and how many activities they are in. So, for us, dropping some items from the schedule was the best thing. My son had less anxiety, I was putting out less money, we were home together more. We found we appreciated the simple things, such as taking our dog out every night for a walk. Those were quality times. I wasn't just rushing him somewhere and dropping him off. There's a lot of positive things that can come out of a separation; you just have to believe it.

Always make a little time for you. ~Mischelle

Helping Kids Grieve

I was very proactive when it came to my son's emotional health. Even though he didn't display any issues, I still had him in the Rainbows program, which was founded in 1983 with a great mission: it is dedicated to being a source of support for children as they grieve and heal from loss, whether from death, divorce, deployment, or other trauma.

You could have your child or children speak to the school psychologist, or a social worker. There is also a program called Banana Splits you may want to look into. It is a school-based children's group for students who have experienced parental divorce or death. It was founded in 1978 by social worker Liz McGonagle. The program supports children, parents, and teachers in schools across the United States.

I recommend participating in these programs, because even if your kids don't seem to have any deep issues surrounding your divorce, these groups show your child they're not alone—that they're not the only kid going through something. Divorce is very normal, and it's good for kids to not feel alone.

A Word about Support Groups

Be careful about the groups you choose to participate in. Many of them are wonderful, but I was a part of one divorce group with members who were quite bitter and angry. That's not good. Think twice before you surround yourself with this kind of energy. You're going to become like the people you spend the most time with, and it's not healthy to steep in negativity.

Yes, you are going to have your down times and dark days. Visit, but don't stay there. And don't harbor resentment. It's very toxic to you, and very contagious. When you are with people who are bashing their ex and are miserable, and can't let go, you'll be the same way. On the other hand, if you're with people who are more emotionally healthy and more positive, you're going to be similar to them.

This caution goes for all support groups. For example, one friend of mine joined a group for parents of autistic children and met people who had been on the journey much longer. Unfortunately, she found they were more negative than the parents who were new. They kept saying,

"As your child gets older, it gets harder." I told her, "You have to leave this group. This is not healthy for you. Don't worry about what's going to happen in ten years, focus on what's going on right now." She left the group and was much happier.

All this being said, there is a huge need for positive support. As I mentioned earlier, I run a Single Moms group on Facebook. Originally, it was just me posting inspirational messages. Then, all of the sudden, I had more than 3,000 group members! People write to me, private message me. There's such a need for support, and not just among people who've been through a divorce. Women in general need the support of other women. We need someone to turn to, someone who is going to be there for us. Everyone's got a million friends on social media, but when it comes to real life, a lot of people are very lonely.

Accelerating Healing and Happiness

Accept the situation for what it is. You must learn to let go of the past. Don't hold onto it, don't look back. Release anger and regret; it's poisonous for your soul. Be in the moment, and look forward to the future. Believe that things will get better.

Happiness is choice, a daily choice. It's a mindset. You can be happy right now, no matter what's going on. Focus on all the good things in your life. I always recommend people get a gratitude journal. I have one for myself. Every day, I write down three things I'm grateful for. It can be something really simple that we usually take for granted such as, "I have food! I have friends, a house to live in. The sun is out today, I have fresh water." It can be something so simple, or something really big. Once you start writing things down on a daily basis and you start thinking about it, you find you're so grateful for seven things instead of three. But unless you focus on them, you won't even notice all the good things around you. What you focus on expands. So, if you focus on the great things in your life, your life is only going to get better, and put you in a better place.

Affirmations can also be very helpful. Write, "I am strong. I am going to get through this." Write it down twenty times each day, so that it gets wired into your brain, into your subconscious.

It takes the same amount of energy to be negative or to be positive. It's your choice. I'm very upfront and direct. Yes, what you're going through *sucks*. But you know what? It's going to be worth it.

Words of Wisdom from a Professional Grief Counselor

To begin, you must understand the definition of grief. Grief is the normal, universal and healthy response that changes one's life. This definition perhaps helps you better understand the intensity and range of emotions you have been experiencing since you made the decision to separate from your husband and/or heard the words "I want a divorce."

Divorce = death with a small d. Therefore, there is grief. Once you have acknowledged a divorce is pending, you begin to grieve. What does that mean?

Are you feeling sad, angry, sullen or alone, or perhaps overwhelmed and not sure of what you are feeling? Have your eating and sleeping patterns changed? Eating too much, too little or making bad food choices? Sleeping too little or too much? Waking many times during the night? Needing to nap by early afternoon? Have you lost your interest in the hobbies and activities you used to love? Notice your focus and concentration is elusive?

It's true! All of these reactions are the manifestations of grief in your body and mind. By now, you have identified at least one of these normal grief responses that you have experienced. So, what can you do? Very little, as it is well understood and documented that you have very little control over grief. Just as you may have had little or no control over the finality of your marriage.

Recall I said grief is "normal," "healthy" and "universal." Therefore, going through (not over, not under, not around) grief is what will heal you from the hurt and pain you are experiencing.

To heal means to become whole again.

You may want your old life back again, but it is over (the marriage, that is). It's also the end of the dreams and hopes you had, perhaps, since you were a young girl. To recognize the reality of the current situation is one of the first "tasks" in healing. It doesn't happen in an instance. As the myriad of emotions come and go, so too the thoughts and reflections of your reality. Over and over, you will question how you could have prevented the divorce, blaming and taking responsibility for all or some part. Yet you may be the one reading this who believes strongly that the divorce was inevitable or purposeful and you're grateful the marriage is over.

However, that doesn't exempt you from grieving. I'm sure you didn't go into marriage with hopes to divorce. You will have to grieve the fantasy of what it might have been.

How long will the grief last?

What if I told you it would be one week to one month for each year you had been in the relationship? Would that help or hurt your hopes of healing quickly? Simply put, there is no timetable. There is no "normal" for the duration or intensity of this grief journey. You must experience the grief in all its excruciating phases.

You will come through this! As many other women before you, you will have the opportunity to learn much about yourself: your weaknesses and your strengths. You will have the added possibility of becoming more compassionate and capable. You will have gained coping skills that may support you with future grief experiences.

What can you control to help yourself process this web of emotions and experiences?

1. Talk to "safe" friends who will not judge you or give you advice.
2. Seek a professional who will do the same (social worker, psychologist, grief counselor or divorce coach) and validate your normal feelings.

3. Read books and articles to learn what others have done to travel this journey successfully.
4. Exercise as it's known to relieve stress.
5. Write whether in a journal or in the form of letters (never to be mailed). It has been proven writing goes deeper than talking. In addition, with the written record you will be able to recognize the changes and growth of your grief journey.

Anger

I'm sure you know women who, years after divorce (sometimes after a death), remain angry. While anger is a normal feeling in the beginning, it will not serve you long-term if it is not processed and let go. This process will require repetitive actions. Here are three simple ways to release anger by yourself:

1. Color: Take a crayon (not a magic marker) and a piece of paper (yesterday's newspaper will do) and start scribbling back and forth rather briskly until you start to slow down naturally. The anger will lessen.
2. Scream: Take a soft pillow (any will do) and, after removing your lipstick, place your face onto the pillow. Now start screaming as loud as you can. Believe me, no one will hear you.
3. Throw: Take ice cubes and head outdoors. Find a brick or metal wall. Throw the ice cubs as hard as possible. Listen to the sound. Yes, it will sound like broken glass. Why take it outside? No melted water to clean up or broken objects. Of course, you can throw a ball as well, but you won't have the sound effects. If you are limited to the indoors, then take a large piece of paper, crush it into a ball and throw it across a room as hard as you can.

What can you control?

Definitely not your emotions nor the speed of healing from your grief. You can control your actions and attitude. Choose healthy food, get as much rest as possible, exercise, seek support that works for you and write! Writing has been proven to go deeper than talking to revisit and release experiences, doubts and feelings.

Okay, you seem to have a handle on this grief. And then, one day you find that you don't want to get out of bed, or go to work, or see or speak to anybody. Or, an extreme might be you don't even want to email or text a friend. So, what should you do? While there is no "should" in dealing with grief, I would encourage you to have a "pity party." It's really okay to take one day and give in to those depressed feelings.

Caution! Beware it doesn't become a daily habit.

> *"No matter how bad your heart is broken,*
> *the world doesn't stop for your grief" ~Faraaz Kazi*

Here's another conundrum: Before the divorce, you had close friends who you might have worked with or socialized regularly. Where is that friend now? Calling less and less, giving advice...or has she totally disappeared? That, too, is a loss (death of a relationship/friendship) and one to be grieved. We call that a secondary loss. It's real, it happens to most people, and it compounds your grief journey.

Children and Grief

Not only are *you* in the throne of a divorce but you have children in the family. How do you support your child(ren) when you can hardly take care of yourself?

1. Keep his/her routine as close to normal as possible.
2. Listen to your child with no judgment, ridicule or advice.
3. Keep the child informed with honesty, appropriate for the age level.

4. Reassure your child of your love and support. A child needs to know that he will remain in home, school, sports or music activities, unless that is not the plan.
5. Encourage your child to start a journal, writing his feelings about the situation.
6. Get professional support for your child.

~Harriet Vogel

Self-Care Saved My Life

When it comes to taking care of yourself and your family, it's all about figuring out where you are now—and starting right there. Everything is not perfect. Nothing is easy. Other single moms get it, and honor that. As single mothers, we are powerful, and we will find and do what we need to be okay.

As you move from a loss to a new life, grow that sense of empowerment and hope within yourself. Your sisters are with you, providing empathy and a spirit of can-do. This season of your life doesn't define you. Celebrate the possibilities and you'll be slaying it in no time. If you're ready to share your story and join the tribe, visit our Sisterhood of Single Moms group on Facebook or email me at info@slayingitbooks.com.

Positive Affirmations and More Self-Care Tips

Live and be in the moment. Be fully present.

Your mind is a powerful thing and you are in control of it. Choose to be happy. Wonderful things will come your way. Your thoughts shape your experience. Negative thoughts are exceptionally damaging. Retrain yourself to see the positive in every scenario.

Enjoy and trust the process. Life is a journey.

Respect, love, accept, and appreciate yourself. Listen and trust your inner wisdom and intuition.

Be willing to forgive yourself and others. Don't judge or blame; release the guilt and shame. Let go of the past and old hurts. Move forward. Forgiveness is a gift to yourself. Set yourself free. Inner peace and harmony are priceless.

Push yourself. Constantly learn and improve. Be flexible – mind, body, and spirit. Invest in yourself. Grow. Follow your dreams and be a dream chaser.

Be thankful of what you have. Live with love and compassion. Love life. What you put out to the universe will come back to you.

You are in charge of your future. You can have the life you want. Don't be a victim of your circumstances. Claim your power to control your destiny. Let go of fears and limiting thoughts. Go outside of your comfort zone.

Don't ask for life to be easier, become stronger.

Speak up for yourself. Release fears and doubts.
Don't take life for granted. Be grateful to be alive. Your body is your temple, take care of it. Create vibrant health. Listen to your body. Aim for wellness in all aspects of your life.

Every problem is an opportunity for growth. There is always a solution.

You are unique and special. Don't compare or compete with others.

Happiness is an inside job. You can't find it in others. It is a conscious choice.

Be kind to the environment. Be in harmony with nature. Love the earth. Love all living things.

Elder are wise and experienced. Listen to them.

People leave you at the right time. Accept it. Allow yourself time to heal.

You are the average of the five people you spend the most time with it. Choose your friends with care. Let go of those who don't support you.

Chapter 3: How to Slay at Parenting

*You are the glue that keeps it all together,
even when you feel like you are falling apart.*

I never had younger siblings, so I never knew how much work kids could be. It's completely different watching someone else's child versus raising your own. Wow—kids are a tremendous amount of work!

The first year of my son's life felt incredibly long. I was constantly exhausted and sleep deprived. I nursed him for 13 months, which meant a lot of the feeding burden was on me. I did try to bottle feed him, but occasionally he would go on bottle strikes. He was a grazer as well. As a result, I felt like a big boob who lived on the couch for a year. I couldn't leave him for long for fear he would scream his head off, and I didn't nurse in public as that is outside of my comfort zone. I have no issue with moms who can do that, it just wasn't for me. I made the typical first mom mistake of leaping each time my son made a sound. Boy, I'm paying for that all these years later!

Why is it kids have the uncanny ability to drive you absolutely crazy? They know how to push your buttons, for sure. Obviously, you love them—that goes without saying. But some days they drive you bonkers and you can't wait until it's their bedtime. Am I all alone in feeling this way? I doubt it! Then, once they are asleep, you feel guilty for feeling this way...until it all happens all over again, LOL. We have *all* had those nights when you have a glass of vino the minute they fall asleep.

Being a mom can be incredibly stressful at times. Add to it a full day of work, errands, meals, homework, baths and bedtime routine—all on your own. My favorite are the nights when you are tired all day and can't wait to go to bed, only to stay up for hours with your mind racing once you actually get the opportunity to sleep. I guess it's the same reason I can never sleep in late. The moment I'm awake, I start thinking of the million things I need to do.

The Reality of Being a Single Mom

My To-Do list is never-ending. I cross one thing off, then add two more. I'm constantly overwhelmed. I often wonder if my life will ever get easier. More likely, I will get stronger. Many of us never thought we would be in this position, especially if you conceived your child in marriage. Being a mom is hard enough. Add to it the single part, and it gets that much harder. Yet single mothers are a fast-growing segment of the population.

First things first: trying to be a "perfect mom" isn't a great idea, regardless of whether you are married or single. Placing too many unrealistic expectations on yourself is a recipe for unhappiness. Don't compare yourself to other moms, just try your best. The most important thing is to love your kids and learn to let things go. I know how hard it is—I'm Type A and had to learn how to do this when I got divorced. I just couldn't do everything and be everything to everyone all the time. And that's okay.

Raising kids is tough! They test your patience on a daily basis. Let's admit it: kids can suck the life out of you sometimes. They are always in some sort of new stage and need something. Even if you were married to a man who didn't help too much prior to your divorce, at least you could run out to the store without having to drag the kids around with you. You had someone backing you up, or someone you could vent to when things got rough. You could get out for a mom's night out without having to pay for a babysitter.

When you're single, it's a whole other story. All of the burden and responsibility falls squarely on your shoulders. You get no breaks or help. We are the ones who have to get the kids ready for school, pack lunches, prepare meals, help with homework, get them ready for bed and try to have some quality time with them. There are only so many hours in a day to get everything done. Plus, you are financially on your own (more on this in the next chapter). Women typically have custody, so they are the ones who worry about childcare and the associated expenses. Men don't have nearly the same amount of stress that we do, generally speaking. Often, they get to be the fun parent. In many cases, the children reside with the mother the majority of the time, so the mother is the one who is worrying about balancing work with home life.

We have to play the good *and* bad guy, and maintain our patience when our kids test us. Our generation has the added concern of too much social media and access to information. It's emotionally and physically draining.

Being a parent is a full-time job. Being a single parent is at least twice the work. You're the one who has to wake up in the middle of the night with a child, and then work a double. I know: it's not easy.

Build the Connection

Now that we've discussed how tough it can be to parent as a single mom, let's talk about the good stuff. People comment all the time on how close my son and I are. From birth, I felt a deep connection with him. I tell my son daily how much I love him and how important he is to me. Building up his confidence and self-esteem is a priority. I praise his positive behavior and try to instill valuable traits in him.

He knows it is completely unacceptable to be mean or tolerate bullying. I tell him it is good to be different than everyone else, to accept people from all races and walks of life. Children learn hatred and prejudice from their parents and surroundings—no one is born being prejudiced. One of my goals is to have my son volunteer with me more often, perhaps at a soup kitchen one holiday so he can learn to appreciate all that he has. I try to expose him to as many new experiences as possible. Children need to learn to be adaptable to new situations and go with the flow.

Children of divorce go through a lot. They need our love and security. They need our presence. We need to be involved in their lives and to make them feel special. They *don't* require expensive toys and gifts, so don't feel guilty about not being able to provide them with material things. As long as their basic needs are met, they will survive.

It's all about boundaries and schedules. ~Janine

My Top Tips for Single Moms:

1. Try to remind yourself to get down on the floor and give your kids five minutes of your undivided attention. Let them control the pace and what you do. If your kids are younger, play a game with them. Don't worry about rules, it's all about quality bonding time. This is not the time to act like a strict disciplinarian. This should be fun time. Enjoy it. Get into it.

2. Develop a routine for you and your family and stick to it. This provides consistency, structure and security.

3. Focus more on quality time over quantity of time. Carve out a certain block each week to have fun with your children with no distractions—this means

technology and electronic devices are off. Emotionally connect with your kids so they feel special and loved.

4. Develop a support community and network of friends you can rely on. Find a good babysitter and join a childcare co-op. You need to rejuvenate and you deserve some adult time.

5. Raise responsible kids and have them help you out. Team work!

6. Again, *don't be so hard on yourself.*

The Conversation

If you're navigating a new separation right now, you'll need to communicate with your kids about what's going on. It shouldn't just be one talk; it's an ongoing conversation. Children need to know, without a shadow of a doubt, that they are *not* the reason for your divorce, nor do they have any control over the situation. Children should never be made to feel guilty about the separation. Never blame a child for your divorce.

Upon first separating, it is ideal if you and your spouse can sit down with the entire family and talk about the upcoming changes you'll all be experiencing. Afterward, you can individually talk to each child to see how they are feeling and if they have any questions or concerns.

It is important to be in tune with your child's response. This is a conversation they will most likely remember for the rest of their lives. Really *listen* to what they have to say and honor their feelings. Reassure them that your love for them is not changing and that you will both still be there for them. Tell your kids you will always be their mom and dad. Keep your explanation simple and at their level. Older kids and teens might not be surprised, and they may have more questions and concerns. Acknowledge and accept their feelings. Be honest and do not give false promises. Be sure to keep your emotions in check and avoid the blame game. Try to use the word "we" so they understand it is a joint decision and that you are still a united front.

My biggest advice: Try to remain cordial with your ex when absolutely necessary. The children will benefit from it. Make sure to not talk badly about their father. Let them figure it out on their own over time. If you can't afford something, don't feel bad about having to tell your children "no," or "Maybe at a different time." Do NOT feel bad about needing "me" time. ~Merri

Co-Parenting: You're Still a Team

Kids need to feel confident their parents will still be able to get along and co-parent properly. Check your local library, bookstore or Amazon for age-appropriate books about divorce. Continue to check in with your kids throughout and after the process to see how they are doing. Many children hold onto the hope that their parents will get back together. Be careful to not fall into the trap of overindulging this idea due to your guilt. Try to keep things as consistent as possible and maintain the same rules and expectations.

One of the best things you can do for your kids is to not fight in front of them or put one another down. This is harmful and can cause long-term emotional issues for children. If you and your spouse cannot get along, it may be a good idea to get a mediator involved, or to go to counseling together so you can learn to put aside your differences and hurts for the sake of the kids. It is going to be a big adjustment for everyone.

Remember to always put your child's needs first. Now is not the time to be selfish. Sometimes it is in their best interest to not do 50-50 time-sharing as it is too much bouncing around. It can be difficult to keep track of where their personal items are and to manage their extracurricular activities. Be flexible and know that in the future, things may change. Stay openminded as to what is best for the kids. Notify the school and teachers of the situation so they can be on the lookout for behavioral issues. Your child might not verbally express their feelings to you to avoid hurting you or disrupting the situation, but these feelings may come out at school. If your ex-husband isn't in the picture, I recommend having positive male role models around for your child. It could be another single dad, a male friend, your own dad, a teacher, a staff member at the local YMCA, a Cub Scout leader, a sports coach, etc.

Being a single mom is twice the work, but also twice the reward.

Working to co-parent effectively is so important. Each relationship is different and each couple is so different. If a spouse cheats, I am sure it makes co-parenting much more difficult. Fortunately, my ex and I rarely fought. That wasn't our style or personality. I highly recommend being mature and adult about things, even if it means being the bigger person often. You don't always have to be right. Choose your battles; you don't need to attend every argument you are invited to. Put your pride, ego and feelings to the side. Your children come first. They need stability, consistency and unwavering love from both parents.

Try to control your emotions. Remember the reason for doing so—your children and their well-being. Keep conversations kid-focused. Do not allow your ex to control your emotions or see your reactions. Stay calm, even if you are furious inside. Breathe. Think of co-parenting as a business arrangement. Make requests instead of demands. Don't bring up past hurts, and be very careful about what you text or post on social media. Anything and everything can be used against you. Be careful who you share your secrets with. Know who you can fully trust.

Your children will never look at you as less for having rough times. They will love you through it. They will admire you more. ~Crystal

Holidays, Birthdays and Parental Access While Co-Parenting

It is a good idea to have a parenting plan figured out and put it in your divorce agreement to avoid issues in the future. You need to decide how you will split custody, if it will be joint, sole, split, shared, alternating, bird's nest or third-party. Where will the child(ren) reside? What days/times will pick-ups and drop-offs take place, by whom and where?

Depending on the parents' work schedules, you may need to be flexible in regards to parental access on birthdays and holidays. Keep in mind the child's educational and extracurricular activities. Decide as early as possible how you will handle your child's birthday; if you will split the day or celebrate every other year on the actual day. Each parent has the right to the child on their own birthday, regardless of whose day it falls upon. If you act out of a place of respect for your ex and love for your child, you will be able to work through the logistics of it all. It doesn't need to be complicated or stressful.

The non-residential parent usually has the right to two non-consecutive weeks during the summer, with plenty of notice given. The parties should split all major holidays as equally as possible. Again, this may have to center around your work schedules. You will also need to agree on where the residential parent can live; usually it is a certain mile radius from the other parent.

My ex does shift work, and has to work holidays unless they fall on his day off. The more senior employees typically get the holidays off, which has made our arrangement much easier. I typically have my son for the actual holiday as a result. I'm very easygoing and, since my son lives with me, I don't mind sharing him with my ex. As your child gets older, allow them to have a say in what they want. I also make sure I get my ex a present from my son for the holidays and his birthday. Remind yourself that this is for your child's sake. How do you think they would feel not having a gift for their parent? Unless your child is driving and has their own money, you really should be considerate of your child and be willing to do this.

I've always had the philosophy that I would never keep my son away from his dad. He could see him any time he wanted as long as it would work out for us and didn't interrupt his routine too much. This approach is for the benefit of the child. Be an adult and share all major decision-making regarding health, education, and the welfare of the child. I always share school events, activities, report cards, and calendars with my son's father. I make sure he gets school photos, knows when there are fundraisers, etc. My ex is the first to know if my son is sick. Keeping the lines of communication open is so important. Be respectful of your ex. Let him know your child's whereabouts, especially if you have residential custody. Inform him of your trips and vacations. The other parent should always have access to your child via phone/text/ Skype, etc.

Another important item I would insist on is this one: do not permit the designation of "mother" or "father" or equivalents to be used by the children with reference to any person other than their natural mother and father. I have seen it done and it really isn't a good situation for anyone.

Figure out how you will handle filing taxes, child care, health insurance and co-pays. Think about what you will do if one parent gets a raise. How will you handle the child support amount? Who will pay for extracurricular activities, camps, tutors, field trip fees, athletic activities, religious events or supplemental educational instruction?

The First Year of Co-Parenting

The first year is definitely the toughest because you are trying to figure it all out. Also, the first year sets the tone. Put your boundaries in place *now*. Be in control in an assertive yet non-bitchy way. Set guidelines but be flexible at the same time. Sometimes your ex might ask for favors; do it if you can because one day you will be needing them yourself. Try to make your relationship as amicable as possible. If you are the custodial parent, try to include your ex in special events and day-to-day news as much as possible.

Judges agree now that having the kids bounce back and forth between each house is not healthy for them. The new trend is one week at one house, the next week at the other. I have my son 24/7, and my ex used to take him every other weekend. Some dads will see the child one day mid-week...it really depends on your work schedules, distance between homes and other logistics. I don't think there is just one "right" way. Let the child have a say (if they are old enough) yet don't let them have total control. Some young children don't want to go to Dad's house and may cry. Try not to give in. That isn't fair to the other parent and the child must learn to go to both (as long as they are safe).

More Tips for Effective Co-Parenting

- Try to be on the same page for rules, discipline, schedule, homework and sleep. If that is not possible, accept the fact that you are each going to choose to parent in your own way. You may not agree with your ex's style, but you do have to accept it. The quicker you can learn to let that control go, the better it will be for you. You can only control yourself, nobody else.
- Never use your children as the middle-man!
- Apologize when you are in the wrong.
- Ask the other parent for their opinion. Let them feel valued.
- Be understanding if your ex is running late for pick-ups or drop offs. Try not to fight over trivial things.
- Compromise at times.
- Respect one another.
- Keep in mind that your ex is hurting too, as well as your child. It isn't easy for anyone!

- Both parents need to have a say when it comes to education, medical needs and financial issues.
- Create a co-parenting plan together. How will you handle holidays and birthdays?

Perhaps most importantly, try to remember the positive traits of the other parent. Your children benefit from having both parents involved. Do the inner work to learn and grow from your failed relationship. Try not to bring those same mistakes into your co-parenting.

The overwhelming theme I always return to when talking to other single mommas is **don't be bitter.** *It occupies energy and space in your heart meant for you and your child. It only hurts you and the child, never the father.* ~Suzy

Dealing with Your Ex

It's always best for the children if you can co-parent with your ex-husband in a healthy manner. No matter how difficult your ex-husband may be, try to put your children's best interests first. Remember that you are the adult, and you need to act like one. Never put your children in the middle of your negative situation, or use them to hurt each other.

Children are the result of your relationship, not the demise of your relationship. Keeping the lines of communication open with your ex-husband at all times is necessary for a separation with children involved. Doing this well is often an exercise of mythic self-control, especially if you sincerely dislike your ex-husband. These are the moments in your life when the strength a woman possesses to dig deep inside will help you prevail.

- Keep your ex-husband informed of important events, issues, concerns, etc.
- Stay positive, and have difficult discussions when the children are not present.
- Treat your child's father as you wish to be treated, even if he doesn't reciprocate. I personally like knowing that I can rest my head on my pillow each night without guilt.

If your ex-husband hurt you in your marriage, learn to let go of the hate and anger for your own sake. I see too many single moms who can't let it go. They are miserable, and most likely making their loved ones miserable as well. Learn to forgive and move forward. Hate and anger will just eat at you until there is nothing left but an empty shell. Don't ever speak poorly about your ex-husband in front of your children. This will only hurt your children. Don't put your children in the middle, either.

Try not to express your fears and stress to your children. Talk to a trusted friend instead. Let your kids be kids. They are too young, and shouldn't worry about finances or other adult problems. They are dealing with enough with the divorce, you don't need to add to their stress. Try to maintain as much normalcy as possible, and limit the amount of shuffling back and forth.

Does my ex-husband drive me crazy at times? Yes, of course. However, I try my very best to not let it get to me, otherwise it will just eat at me. This takes an immense amount of control on my part to not respond in a way that I will regret. I don't allow him to see or know how much he bothers me. That would just be letting him win. Over time, I have learned to accept him for who he is. I have little expectations for him. I realize now that I am in control of my emotions and reactions, he does not have that sort of control over me. You can never blame anyone else for your behavior or emotions.

Again, you never fully know a person till you divorce them. It's astounding how completely different a person can treat you, post-marriage. I remember one of my girlfriends telling me to not be ignorant with divorce. I had no idea what she meant till I personally went through it and made all the typical novice mistakes that newly separated women do. Never say your ex-husband isn't capable of acting a certain way or doing something. Don't be dumb, ladies. I have seen it over and over again where the men take action first and have the upper hand. Be proactive and smart, otherwise you will lose out and suffer.

Feelings and Stress

Most children struggle with divorce, albeit in a different way from adults, even if they don't express their feelings or fears to you. Children are far more intuitive than parents acknowledge, especially when saturated with the stress of a divorce. Children know, even if on a basic level, that both parents are experiencing pain, that a change is about to happen (or has happened). Sometimes, children don't know if they were the cause, or if they could have provided the solution. That's too much imposed stress for a child who didn't do anything wrong, and it's the main reason to keep communicating and reassuring them. Kids aren't dumb. They feel things. Even if you're not fighting, there's still tension.

A child doesn't deserve to feel the burning debris from an exploding marriage. It's easy to overlook children feeling sympathy pains or guilt when a dense fog envelopes you, and you have no idea which direction to travel. It's these moments when you show your child what it means to be strong. Your child will see that you don't know the answer, and you are in pain, but you are choosing to triumph by remaining strong and never giving up. By watching the decisions you make and the people you turn to for help, your child will learn how to reach out for support when needed, and how to provide support whenever possible. What a powerful lesson! On the next page, you will see advice from a Licensed Therapist regarding how best to help your children.

Advice from a Licensed Therapist

Going through a divorce can be incredibly challenging for everyone involved. It's an emotional roller-coaster which can commonly include stress, depression, decreased life satisfaction, financial stressors, and anxiety. Not only is there the adjustment of getting used to being single again, there is also the divorce process itself. The often long, drawn out legal process constantly offers reminders of why the marriage failed in the first place. Add into the mix child custody issues if children are involved, and the process can turn into a complete nightmare.

Depending on the circumstances for the divorce, women are commonly left devastated and feeling like failures. Married individuals (especially women) often get much of their personal sense of identify from their marital status and often self-identify as wives and mothers. Most women marry expecting to be married to their partners for their entire lifetime. They plan on starting and raising a family together, creating a lifetime of happy memories, and eventually growing old together. A divorce brings that life dream to a crashing halt. It can be a traumatic experience. As a result, going through a divorce can often leave women feeling like they've completely lost themselves.

So, what can you do to help yourself heal from this traumatic experience? You have to learn to focus on yourself. At first you may feel broken and as if the world is collapsing around you, but I assure you this is something you can handle. You are stronger than you ever imagined. It's time to get your priorities straight. You, my dear, are the most important person in your world. You begin by learning to love yourself unconditionally. It should always be "me" before "we."

When you love yourself unconditionally, everything falls into place. When you love yourself unconditionally, there is no room for depression, fear, anxiety, and all of the other emotions that weigh you down.

What does it really mean to love yourself unconditionally?

It is to love yourself without conditions, with no strings attached. It is to accept yourself as you are in this moment. To accept all parts of yourself: the good, the bad, and the parts of yourself that you keep hidden. When you learn to love yourself unconditionally, you become one with the essence within you. You step into your power and become the magnificent being you were placed on this earth to be. Once you learn this skill, you will not only **S.H.I.N.E.** but you will be the best version of yourself. So how do you do it? I'm not going to sugarcoat it. I will be brutally honest: this is not an easy journey. You may doubt yourself a million times along this journey. But I promise you it will be worth it.

By doing these eight essential things, you can begin your journey to loving yourself and healing after a divorce.

1. **Self-Care:** Make self-care a daily practice because you are worth it. Make the relationship with yourself a priority each and every day. Self-care is any act that helps you feel recharged and centered: mind, body, and spirit. It's not about forcing yourself to do something you hate but taking care of yourself mind, body, and soul.

> **Mind:** Take time to create a healthy internal dialogue. If you have negative thoughts about yourself or your body, it's okay. Don't shame yourself. Did you know the brain is biologically wired to think negative thoughts? You just have to re-train the brain, so to speak. Be compassionate with yourself. If you struggle with this, know it just means you have some things that need to be cleared out.

> **Body:** Move your body in a loving way. Forcing yourself to do something you hate will not stick for long. Do what you love, and it won't feel like a workout. Nourish your body with healthy foods. Do not starve yourself or go on the latest starvation diet. Nourish your body with healthy foods most of

the time and if you slip, don't shame yourself. It's about balance and helping your body thrive.

Soul: Do what sets your soul on fire. Make time to play, have fun, and let loose. These are probably the best moments you will ever have. Create a little bit of this every day. You cannot be your optimal self if you do not take care of yourself. Taking care of others comes easy, but making ourselves a priority is usually left on the back burner. Change your mindset: SELF-CARE is not an indulgence but an everyday necessity.

2. **Get to know the real you**: Really get to know yourself on a soul level. What do you enjoy? What makes you feel playful? What do you crave more of? Once you know, start doing these things and watch the magic happen.

3. **Let go of perfectionism**: Being perfect is so overrated and exhausting. This can also be linked to trying to please others. Give yourself permission to make a mistake.

4. **Embrace your insecurities**: Stop wishing you were different. You are an amazing person who was placed on this earth for a purpose. If you haven't found it yet, don't give up. Be gentle with yourself. Stop beating yourself up. First identify what causes you to feel this way. Is it really about the present situation? If not, when in the past do you remember feeling this way? If you identify past issues, this is an indicator that you may have unresolved trauma. See **step 5** for advice on this.

5. **Confront your past**: You must have the courage to confront what brought you here in the first place. It's about being brutally honest about what has caused those deep emotional scars and beginning to peel back the layers a little at a time. Eventually, you begin to trust the process and you will have the strength to feel it, acknowledge it, forgive, and then let it go. This is not always an easy process, but it is life-changing. Also keep in mind that a divorce can trigger old wounds that have not yet been healed. The reason behind it is that the brain

wires together experiences that provoke similar feelings. An example: let's say as a child you experienced a traumatic car accident where you lost a loved one. You felt sad, alone, angry, guilty, and resentful as a result of this event. If you never really dealt with these feelings, they are unresolved. As you go through life experiencing other events with these feelings, your brain wires them together. And then, you go through a divorce. The intensity of the feelings is completely overwhelming because it is not just about your relationship ending but a pileup, if you will, of a lifetime of similar feelings.

Don't be ashamed to reach out for professional help. Giving yourself support along the way is one of the greatest gifts you can give yourself and your children if you are a mother. Your children can pick up on your stress level even when you think you are hiding it. You cannot be emotionally available to your children when you are overwhelmed, dealing with the roller-coaster of emotions. Going through a divorce sometimes leaves you feeling like you are losing your mind.

It is best to work with an experienced licensed mental health professional when addressing divorce and serious issues such as trauma. The reason behind this is you may not have the support and tools you need to confront your past trauma. Don't try to do it alone. An experienced licensed mental health professional will teach you the tools needed so you can begin to address the trauma in more manageable parts.

6. **Nurture your inner feminine side**: Make time to have fun, be playful, and sexy. Take time to connect with the divine feminine side of yourself. Do the things that set your soul on fire!

7. **Realize your strength**: Just the fact that you were able to make it through is proof enough that you are one of the most resilient and amazing humans alive. You've already made it past the most difficult part. Take the lessons and know you can make it through anything.

8. **Acknowledge your negative voice**: Listen for a moment to what the negative voice in your head is saying. It has really just been trying to

protect you all this time. Normally it is developed in childhood to avoid pain and keep you safe. Remember that it is a fear-based response. Respond in a compassionate way by acknowledging it and thanking it for keeping you safe all this time. Then reassure it that you have the situation under control.

Tips for Helping Your Children

One last thing to consider: A divorce impacts everyone in the family. If children are involved, here are a few tips to consider. If you and your ex are going to effectively co-parent, mediation by a family/couple's therapist may be greatly beneficial. The therapist will teach you the skills to co-parent in the most effective way and learn to be civil toward one another for the sake of your children. Both parents must be willing to put in the work for this to work most effectively. If your ex is refusing, try on your own. It can't hurt to learn the skills yourself and do what is best for your child/children. Try even when it feels like you are the only one putting in the effort. Your child will thank you one day.

Also, pay close attention to your children. Sometimes children talk about their feelings but more commonly than not, children act out their feelings. So, expect the misbehavior, changes in moods or temperament. Every child will respond differently. Children experience a sense of powerlessness and loss when their parents separate. Getting support for yourself can help your child cope more effectively through the divorce. If your child notices that you are coping, they tend to be less anxious. On the other hand, if there is hostility and ongoing conflict between you and your partner, it will also make it more difficult for your child to cope. Ongoing conflict and hostility may cause your child/children to experience behavioral and emotional concerns.

Follow these recommendations to help your child/children cope:

- Tell them both parents love them and reassure them that although your family is changing, they will not lose your love and they will continue to be cared for.

- Be sure to give undivided attention to each child as much as possible, as your actions speak louder than words.

- Be sure to explain any changes that may happen in your child's life such as where they will be living, who they will spend weekends with. Be very clear as to what will change and what will remain the same.

- Try to keep your child's routines in place as much as possible.

- Allow your child to ask questions and promote healthy dialogue about the changes in your family. Be sure to only include appropriate details. This will help your child feel safe in coming to when they need emotional support.

- Going back and forth between two homes can be difficult for children. Provide extra support before and after visits with the other parent.

- Recognize that if your child is struggling emotionally and behaviorally, it is important to get support for them as well. Find a child therapist who can help them process the changes in their family. Even if your child is little, there are many modalities that exist that don't even require your child to talk to benefit from therapy.

- Keep in mind that most children deep down dream that their parents will get back together. So, if you decide to start a new relationship, understand that this may have a negative impact on your child, at least initially. Seeking counseling can help you learn the best way to introduce this new change to your child.

Changes of any kind are hard; know that you will get through it. If you have children, they will get through it as well. Children are resilient and can make it through just about anything with the appropriate level of support. Seek support in the form of counseling so both you and your child/children have the appropriate skills to cope with all of the changes.

~Janet Garcia, LCSW, EMDR Certified Therapist

Organizations Providing Support

As I mentioned earlier, many schools and churches offer Banana Splits and Rainbow programs for children of separated, divorced, or widowed families. Big Brothers and Big Sisters of America is another great place to turn. It's an organization with a longstanding rate of success, run with the belief that children deserve every opportunity to thrive. It recognizes child safety as an utmost priority.

Another great organization is the Boys & Girls Club. It is a safe place for children to learn and grow while having fun instead of being left unsupervised to get into trouble. Boys & Girls Clubs offer programs and services to promote and enhance the development of children in a safe and structured environment, where they can develop a sense of competence, usefulness, belonging and influence. Many schools offer before and after school programs for working parents. Homework assistance is available by the staff and they offer various programs for the students.

4-H programs are another option to explore. These groups empower young people to lead for a lifetime. They have programs in science, healthy living and citizenship. 4-H offers camps, after-school programs, in-school activities, and clubs.

It is important for males, in particular, to feel like they belong to something. My son and I did Cub Scouts together, even though it is traditionally a father/son thing. I enrolled him in martial arts and he had a male instructor. Boys need healthy male role models in their lives. They need to see a good man regularly to know how to become one. As they get older, provide opportunities for your children to join positive groups (church, sports, clubs) instead of letting them fall prey to gangs or cults.

My son doesn't do as many activities right now as he did before the divorce, but we have more downtime and quality time together now. I believe parents enroll their children in too many organized activities, causing them to burn out at an early age. In particular, parents put too many expectations on their children when it comes to sports. Children feel an intense amount of pressure to excel at sports at a young age. This is part of the reason why this generation is full of stress and anxiety. Parents need to stop trying to entertain every hour of their child's life. Children should be bored at times, and learn how to entertain themselves. As a parent, we must be cautious about trying to live through our children.

Though you may feel as if you are alone, sinking in quicksand, you have actually never been closer to help. Take responsibility for yourself and for your children's happiness. Cause your family to succeed despite any obstacles, and achieve that milestone by accepting the nonstop, overwhelmingly helpful and affordable options and programs available to everyone.

If you have time to post pictures and updates on Facebook, Twitter, or any social media sites, then you have time to research how to create a better life for you and your family. Don't be a person who sits and complains, be a person who takes action and has accountability. If you are feeling overwhelmed or depressed, it is imperative you get the counseling and support that you need. Do not rely on your kids for support. Instead, use a trusted friend or therapist.

I only did the single parenting thing for two years, but my advice would be to accept that you cannot do everything and be all. Something's gotta give.

There will be mothers who have time and patience to show up for every extracurricular activity, willingly take on volunteer jobs and participate in the bake sale. I did not have the capacity for this, and in retrospect, I wish someone had told me that it is okay to use the "I am a single-parent card" to get out of a few things. ~Catrin

Parenting & Technology

It kills me to see parents on their cell phones all day long, ignoring their kids. You even see it at the playground. A few years from now, you won't even remember what you were looking at on your phone, but you will miss those moments with your kids that you can't get back. Your phone will always be there, but your kids are constantly changing. As your kids get older, they will become more interested in their friends and doing things on their own. Cherish their younger days because they will be older before you know it.

Kids mirror their parents. Even when you think they are not looking or listening, they are really taking it all in. If you are on your electronic devices 24/7, I can pretty much guarantee your kids will be, too. I see kids starving for the attention of their parents who are too occupied on their phones or laptops. While it is great for kids to know how to use technology, it is not good for it take over their lives. I recommend holding off on introducing your kids to all the latest gadgets. They will have plenty of time to catch up.

There is a major disconnect going on in our society. Technology has taken over. While it has its benefits, it also causes people to lose that crucial personal connection with one another. You rarely hear about weekly family dinners. People have hundreds of so-called friends on Facebook, but in their day-to-day lives, they are extremely lonely and isolated. It is probably part of the reason so many marriages and relationships fail.

We need to return to old times, when families spent quality time together and enjoyed one another. If we don't show our children what healthy behavior is, then they will not know how to have a healthy relationship when they are adults. Your childhood has a tremendous impact on your adulthood. As a parent, it is your responsibility to model positive behavior. Kids only know what they see and experience firsthand. Kids will not listen to your words, but rather your actions. Kids must learn how to interact with peers and adults in the real world, not just the cyber world.

> *The phone will always be there, your kids won't. Make time for them now while they still want you to.*

Spoiling

Single parents tend to have guilt and overcompensate by spoiling their children. I think we have to be careful about overdoing this. Too many children have a sense of entitlement because we give and do way too much for them. They do not know the value of money or how to wait for things. This generation is accustomed to instant gratification. We don't make them wait or earn things. One thing I have zero patience for is whining. In my opinion, my son is too old to whine. Sometimes I will whine back to him just to be annoying. Hey, I have to have some fun at parenting!

Children are also overstimulated with all their technological devices. They no longer know what it's like to be bored because they are shuffled from one activity to the next. They have experienced organized play dates their entire lives. Sadly, not many kids play outside anymore. They lack social skills because they are spending more and more time on electronic devices. There is less family and peer interaction as a result of electronics. This is not healthy.

We put too much emphasis on kids and allow them to control our lives. In some cases, kids do not respect their parents or authority. They definitely do not fear teachers anymore, and gone are the days when they dreaded going to the Principal's office. Children have access to too much information thanks to social media.

The last generation of parents were strict, so I think we swore to never be like our parents. We went to the extreme and many parents are allowing kids to have too much say and freedom, which causes friction at home with families. We've made the mistake of trying to be their friend instead of their parent. We try too hard to make them happy and to ensure they have an easy life, which does a disservice to them in the long run. Children need and want boundaries and rules set by their parents. Giving them chores and responsibilities will pay off in the future. Life should not be centered around kids. The adults need to take care of themselves and their relationship first to provide a solid family foundation.

I am trying to instill independence, responsibility, and politeness in my son. We need more gentlemen in the world, with old fashioned values. All you have is your character, so it's imperative I model appropriate values, ethics, and morals. I stress the importance of health, happiness, and education. Even though I am no longer married, I do want my son to know it's wonderful to be in a healthy, happy relationship. I enjoy it when he goes on playdates and sees happy families. I don't want him to think being single is the only way to be.

> ***Your children are your greatest masterpiece.***

The Decision to Be Happy

Life most certainly doesn't always work out the way you think it should! But happiness is still possible. Sometimes, Plan B works out better than Plan A. To avoid being miserable, accept your situation and make the most out of it. We either make ourselves miserable or we make ourselves stronger based on our thoughts. The amount of work is the same and the choice is yours.

Life is short, so I'm certainly not wasting my time and energy on being negative and blaming others for my unhappiness. Life is what *I* make of it. Plain and simple, no one's life is perfect, no matter how good it might look from the outside. It's funny how you have this idea or image of what your life will be, and what your husband and children will be like. Only God (or your personal higher power) really knows what's in store for you.

To be happy, you need to appreciate what you have been given and not mourn what you thought would be. If you can't appreciate and be happy with what you currently have, what makes you think you will appreciate and be happier with more? Live in the present, and appreciate everything you have and all the wonderful people in your life who love you. There is no need to think about the past— it's behind you. There's no need to worry about the future; you don't have control over it. Worrying doesn't help you at all, so why do it? Learning to accept where you are at this very moment and just *being* is what will allow you to be happy.

> *Even on your bad days, your kids still think you are the best mom in the universe.*

Advice from People Raised by Single Parents

Don't speak ill of your ex to your kids. It will make them feel bad about themselves.

Make sure your kids know they are important and that you will never leave them. Kids fear this.

Never pick a man over your kids. Be careful about introducing men to your kids too quickly—there's no need to involve your kids in every guy you date.

Teach your kids appropriate hygiene, teen issues, and behavior.

Make time for your kids no matter how busy or tired you are. It doesn't cost anything to give them your presence and love. Quality time vs. quantity.

Remember, this too will pass. The difficulties you are enduring now will only last for a short time. Keep a healthy perspective on life.

Life is what you make of it. Don't give darkness power.

Don't drag out the divorce.

Take time to make a life, not just a living.

Be a good role model.

Listen to your kids and their feelings. Show your kids they are important, pay attention to them.

Help your kids in school, try to attend their activities.

Seek guidance and help when needed.

Tell your children the reason for your divorce in an age appropriate way. Communicate about the divorce; be honest within reason.

Teach your children you don't need to rely on a romantic partner to thrive. Work hard for what you want and teach your kids you don't ever need to stay in a bad relationship.

Get along with your ex for your kid's sake.

Take care of yourself! If mom isn't happy, how can the kids be happy?

Show your kids what a healthy, happy relationship looks like.

Don't leave your kids alone at too young of an age.

Teach kids healthy eating. Don't live on fast food. The habits we create as parents echo through our children.

Don't use children as pawns.

When the child is older, let them decide who they want to live with.

Act as the parent and not their friend. Don't make your kids into an adult too soon. That's not fair to them.

Chapter 4: Work and Finances

You can survive anything. Keep going.

During my separation and divorce, I made a conscious decision to take the high road and act like a mature adult. I am not saying I am perfect or that I always made the right choices throughout, but my goal was to have it be as smooth as possible for everyone involved. I didn't want things to get ugly or for it to be dragged out. I figured in the long run you attract more bees with honey, so it made sense all around to be amicable.

We really didn't have much to argue over, anyway. We didn't have investments, multiple houses, etc. My ex has a government job so it's not as if he could hide anything from me, nor could he do anything illegal without being thrown in jail. I had it very easy in comparison to others. I have heard too many stories of husbands who work off the books and don't report money to spite their wives. I never had to deal with any of that ridiculousness. We basically split everything down the line. We paid off our debt and moved forward with our lives. I didn't fight him on anything in particular, and it was smooth sailing for the most part.

I chose to give up a lot of my rights in order to have my freedom and live life on my terms. I always had the mindset that money can be made. I am college educated, have street smarts and don't mind hustling. Plus, I always knew I had my mom's support if I needed it. I was fortunate in many ways, and I was aware of it. This is not to say my life is easy or perfect, because I definitely still struggle. I had to reinvent myself after my divorce. I went back to work and got additional training. I saw the value of investing in myself and my future. I looked at the whole picture and made a plan to achieve long-term gains.

Of course, there are times when I wonder if I gave in too easily—if I should have fought for certain things. Life is expensive and you can't rely on Social Security to be there for you when you get older. I gave up some big-ticket items, but I told myself you can't put a price tag on peace and freedom. Plus, I could have married someone who didn't have as much as my ex did. Life post-divorce has been financially challenging for me, but it has also provided the hunger and drive to succeed on my own.

Some of my closer friends who knew the details of my circumstances thought I was crazy to not fight. I never stepped foot in a court; I told myself I wasn't going down that path. I didn't want to become bitter like so many divorcees I see. Life is too short. Perhaps some of it is my belief in my higher power; knowing that He is taking care of me.

I also force myself not to let my mind consume itself with future worries. All I can do is live for today and plan for the future. I'm putting in the time now so hopefully it will pay off in the future. I want to be proud of myself, knowing that I provided for my son.

I don't want to rely on a man for financial reasons. I have big dreams for us. I want to be the hero of my own story. Does my life have a lot of uncertainty? Yes, most definitely. Do I get stressed out financially? 100%. I can honestly say I now understand how people become homeless; life is way more expensive than I ever realized. I gave up a cozy lifestyle as a stay-at-home mom. I really didn't have too many worries or financial stress. My life completely changed after my divorce. I get scared about my future, but one thing I know for sure is that I will *never* sell myself short.

> *Always remember that even when you feel like it's never enough it always is. Some days are better than others, but in the end, your kids will know you did your best. ~Brittiny*

The Corporate Jungle

If you were a stay-at-home mother prior to your divorce, it may prove difficult to get back into the workforce after all those years off. It's a corporate jungle out there. If you've been out there interviewing, it can feel like companies prefer to hire a recent graduate at a lower rate instead of a qualified mom at a higher rate. We put ourselves at a disadvantage when we choose to stay home and raise our children instead of working. We put our careers on hold.

When moms return to the workforce, even though they have college degrees and years of experience, many have no choice to but to obtain a job at a lower level than the position they occupied before having kids. It's technically illegal for a prospective employer to ask personal questions, but many do it anyway. They want to know if you are married, have children, etc. They prefer to hire someone who won't be needing to leave early, or take days off to take care of the kids. Men rarely have to worry about a potential employer asking those types of questions, nor do they deal with those issues. Life most certainly is not fair.

Flexible Work Opportunities

In real estate, the most important thing is location, location, location. For single moms, the most important job criterion is flexibility, flexibility, flexibility. It's ideal to find a job that you can schedule around your family life. I have come up with some job categories that fit the bill. Getting into real estate, in fact, may be a good option as it is relatively inexpensive in terms of training required. You can create your own hours, choose when to meet with clients, and host open houses. You can work from your computer or cell phone at home at hours that are convenient for you.

I suggest looking at fields that require little capital to get into, such a direct sales companies, affiliate marketing, blogging, website design, healthcare, and medical transcription. Teaching offers many options, such as virtual video lessons, tutoring and freelance work. There is a website called tutoring.com you may want to explore. You fill out the form, and if they find an opportunity that fits your request, they will notify you. If you are artistic or crafty, you can sell your handmade items on sites like Etsy, eBay, and at local arts and craft festivals. Another artistic field is graphic design. You can work right from your home computer.

Some companies hire freelance customer service representatives who can work from home. You will need a separate phone line and computer, as well as a quiet work area. This is best for moms who work while their kids are in school. Bookkeeping and tax preparation are other services you can offer if you are knowledgeable in those fields. Many people make full time income with online freelancing. Think outside of the box and explore your options.

Here are a few more ideas for you:

- Financial planner
- Interior designer
- Hairdresser
- Makeup artist
- Server
- Nurse
- Fitness instructor
- Librarian
- Dental hygienist
- Nanny

No matter which field you decide to pursue, balancing work and home life is a job in itself, which single moms already know. I urge you to try to find something where you have control over your schedule, so you don't burn out. At the end of the day, however, you'll do what you have to do to support your family.

If you choose to work for a company, make sure they are family friendly and understanding of your situation. If you're having a difficult time finding a good job, try a local employment placement agency. I find asking around is the best way to find out about jobs. Word of mouth and referrals go a long way. Often, you find out about jobs from your friends and family. LinkedIn is another great tool to use when job searching. Check out workingmother.com for their yearly list of the 100 Best Companies for working mothers. These companies offer a broad array of support, from flexible work hours to mentoring, affordable childcare and paid leave. Look online at Monster, Snagajob, Indeed, CareerBuilder, ZipRecruiter, and Craigslist. Don't be afraid to tell your friends, family, neighbors and anyone you know that you are job hunting. You may be surprised at who can hook you up with something. You won't know unless you ask.

You can find companies that will work around holidays and school schedules. All Chick-fil-A restaurants, for example, are closed for business on Sundays, as well as Thanksgiving and Christmas. You can do a search on Google and see what companies turn up. When my son was young, I worked as an assistant teacher at his nursery school. This way, I was able to work around his school schedule, which made my life much easier to coordinate. Even though my salary was not high at the nursery school, I didn't have to pay for a sitter. When looking for a job, be sure to take various factors into consideration. One year, I was a nanny and was able to bring my son with me. He took the bus with the children to school, so it worked out perfectly. Try to be open and creative regarding your career options.

Regardless of the direction you choose, believe in yourself and your ability to be successful and thrive in your career. Break through your self-limiting beliefs and become the person you want to be. Follow your dreams, and don't let being a single mom be your excuse not to reach them. You deserve to have a life of abundance and feel proud of all you have accomplished. Be careful about the story you are telling yourself—it will likely come true.

> *Don't pity me because I am a single mum. Respect me for having the courage to do it alone, the strength to never give up, and the love to put my child's needs before my own. ~Crystal*

A Word of Caution

You must be careful with certain online sites such as Craigslist. Sadly, there are many unethical people out there who will try to scam you out of money. *Never* wire money to anyone you do not personally know. Avoid shipping out items to people you do not know. The safest way to avoid losing money is to only work with local people that you can meet in person. Do not accept cashier/certified or money orders. If they are fake, your bank will make you responsible for the amount.

Some individuals will post fake jobs claiming they will wire you money for your services. Never give out any of your private financial information, such as bank account numbers, Social Security numbers, PayPal account or credit card numbers. Do not make a payment for a rental that you have not seen in person.

Use your common sense. If something sounds too good to be true, it is most likely a scam or a fraud. Trust your gut feeling and be sure to notify the Internet Fraud Complaint Center if you fall prey to one. Do not feel ashamed or embarrassed; these people are extremely tricky and make a living out of scamming innocent people. They are professional con artists.

Advice from a Tax Professional

My biggest caution to those who are newly or recently divorced is the IRS does not follow what is in the divorce decree as to who claims the child as a dependent. The number one rule for who gets to claim the child is: whose house did the child sleep at most? As in *actual overnight stays.* Custody will never be completely equal, because there are 365 days in a year; someone will have the child more. I tell my clients, "Keep a calendar as to the nights your child slept at your house in case it's ever contested." If your divorce decree says the other parent gets to claim the child, you need to provide the non-custodial parent with a form 8332.

If the client was a stay-at-home mom, unless they started working as soon as the divorce happened, there's really no specific forms they would have to account for at tax time. The only thing that would change is alimony payments or child support. There is a difference between the two. Child support is nontaxable no matter what. Alimony payments are taxable income, but will no longer be considered taxable for divorces starting in 2019. The change simplifies things in some situations. But for the ones who have to pay it, they're no longer happy.

Don't Wait to Speak to a Tax Pro

I would definitely advise both parties going through a divorce talk with a tax expert, during and after a divorce. Divorce has significant implications with respect to allowable credits, along with the financial aspects of life in general. While we are tax experts, we can also help our clients ensure their financial needs are being taken care of, sending them to other professionals if needed. I work with a few clients to make sure their budgets are in place, and things they need to think about, such as:

- Who is going to take care of your child when you are at work? What will that cost?

- How are the kids going to get to school?
- What are your added costs in food prep? If you begin working, you're going to be more tired than you used to be. You need to budget in the cost of easier meals or that McDonald's stop.
- Gas
- Tolls

It all adds up. Failing to account for a changing budget and forgetting to update their W-2 withholdings are two common mistakes newly single people make. If you forget to update your withholdings, when tax season comes, you may get hit with a tax bill or a lower refund than you were expecting.

Communicate

While divorces are tough, I definitely advise communicating during and after with your spouse about your taxes and what you're going to do—especially that first year. That first year is always the hardest as to who is claiming the kids. If both of you claim the kids, your refund can get held up. In addition, only the person who has the kids the most, more than 50% of the time, gets to claim the Earned Income Tax Credit.

For those single mothers who earn income via MLM sales, my advice is to keep an accurate inventory. Without it, you can't take the expense in the year you buy your products; you can only take it in the year you sell the products.

When people are going through a divorce, I think it's a good idea to give me—or another tax professional—a call. That way, we can talk through the financial implications and the tax implications right away so you can keep accurate records from the beginning.

~ Michelle Zambos-Duerksen, AFSP

Time to Talk Money!

You might feel uncomfortable talking about finances with others. I get it. Just the mere *thought* of your financial situation can be scary and overwhelming. According to the U.S. Census Bureau, single mothers have the lowest median income of any family type. We worry about childcare, housing, clothing (we all know how fast kids grow out of clothes), extracurricular activities, birthdays, and holidays. Food and gas alone eat up much of my budget.

If you are having trouble making ends meet, do not feel ashamed. The U.S. Government understands the challenges single mothers face. They have created grants to help with credit card debt, and state programs to help you with everyday bills. For specific agencies and resources, look at the end of this chapter for a list of where to begin.

Research your options. Seek out government assistance for your food and health insurance needs. You will need to meet some requirements in order to qualify, and there are deadlines and certain timelines you must follow. Be sure to get all the necessary information so you don't miss out. There are way too many grants for me to list and discuss, so I recommend doing a search online for your particular needs. There are also grants for female business entrepreneurs. Don't allow lack of money to prevent you from making your dream happen.

Do whatever it takes to survive, and make sure you fight for your child support. I know many women who are supposed to get support from their exes but don't. (I honestly don't know how these men live with themselves.) Sadly, many dead-beat dads exist. If you were a mom who stayed at home to raise your children while you were married, I urge you to immediately start planning for your future and retirement. Talk with a financial planner or advisor who can steer you in the right direction.

Breathe and trust in yourself that what once took two together CAN be done by oneself. ~Sarah

Accepting Help

Some moms are fortunate to get financial support from their families, but that often comes with a price tag. Sometimes people try to control others with money. They like to hold it over you. You might feel obligated to do what your family tells you to do. They will give you their unsolicited opinion as to how to raise your child. They may try to tell you how you can spend the money, and how to live your life. While having financial assistance is great, it can also prevent you from being independent. There is something to be said for paying your own bills and living your life the way you want to.

Educate Yourself

As single mothers, we need to become more financially savvy and educated. Being proactive in making extra money while keeping expenses as low as possible is easier said than done, I know. Dave Ramsey is a terrific source for financial advice. A great place to begin is write out a budget for each month and track your expenses. There are many apps and websites that can help you get on track.

Your education is important to your success. The government also offers many grants for schooling. To apply for financial aid, simply start the process with the Free Application for Federal Student Aid (FAFSA).
You do not need to stay in a dead-end job that you hate. The government offers special training programs to help single moms get better jobs, ones that they will actually enjoy. They are even grants to cover your daycare expenses.

Cutting Back & Saving

I highly recommend you use your alimony wisely, and try to save a portion of it for an emergency fund. It's amazing how quickly you can run through that money. As my financial planner advised me, think of it as being in survival mode the first few years after your divorce. It will take some time to get back on your own two feet again, but you will get there. Be smart about how you spend your money, and don't live outside of your means. You don't want to find yourself in debt. For even more guidance and specific information from Amy at Thrivent Financial, turn to the first Appendix at the end of the book.

> *Be proud of yourself. Stand tall.*
> *You've got this, momma!*

One of the hardest parts of dealing with finances, for me, was downsizing my home, my lifestyle, and my son's lifestyle. In time, I realized home is where your heart is—it doesn't matter the size of the house, but rather the people in the home. I try my best to provide for my son so he doesn't feel the financial difference, but of course, our situation is no longer the same. We went from two adults splitting one set of bills, to two adults paying for two sets of bills. I can no longer afford to buy my son everything he wants, but that's a good thing. He isn't as sheltered now, and I'm teaching him how to be money savvy. He values things more, and is more conservative with his finances as a result. My son has his own pet sitting business and sells his old toys online for money. I'm proud of his initiative and drive. He is less spoiled than he used to be. I notice that he asks for few material things.

One of the scariest parts of being a single mom is thinking about my future and security. Since I was a stay-at-home mom for many years, I don't have a pension or retirement fund. I worry about things like this now that I'm getting older. Will I still be working when I'm 70, or even older? Now *that* is a depressing thought. Who will take care of me when my son is grown and has a family of his own? When these thoughts start running through my mind, I try to squash them because some things are honestly too scary to think about. I try to focus on the excitement of the unknown future. My life will be what I make of it.

Financial Resources for Single Moms

1. Start with the TANF program in your state: www.acf.hhs.gov/ofa/help. TANF specifically helps needy families, so kids must be present in the home to qualify for cash benefits.

2. The Single Parents Alliance of America, found at https://www.spaoa.org, is a great resource. You can check your eligibility for support and assistance as well as reduced rates for services such as phone plans.

3. If your family needs reduced cost or free diapers, visit the nationaldiaperbanknetwork.org/need-diapers-now.

4. Still breastfeeding? You may qualify for WIC (women, infants and children) assistance: www.fns.usda.gov/wic/women-infants-and-children-wic.

5. Search for the nearest federal or state-funded Child Care Resource & Referral program by ZIP code here: childcareaware.org/ccrr-search-form/. Your family may qualify for scholarships and grants for daycare and after-school programs.

6. Use the SNAP screening tool to see if you qualify for any supplemental nutrition assistance programs in your state or area: www.snap-step1.usda.gov/fns/.

7. Search for low-income housing availability or pre-qualify for vouchers through the HUD program, which has specific assistance programs just for single mothers: www.verywellfamily.com/housing-assistance-programs-for-single-mothers-2997420.

8. For local and state-level benefits, call 211 or 311 and ask about whatever resources you may need help with. These resources vary greatly depending on where you live, but may include heating oil, coats, cheap/free healthcare programs, flu shots for uninsured/underinsured kids, etc.

Advice from a Certified Financial Planner

If you've ever flown on a plane, you've heard the flight attendant tell you, "If there's a decrease in cabin pressure the oxygen mask will release from the ceiling." They instruct you to put *your* mask on first before placing it on your child. This can be true when we talk about your finances and being a mom. You cannot help others effectively if you don't first take care of yourself. You need to make sure your financial health is good first before you can be in a position to give back. So how to you attain that?

First of all, money is a tool to be used wisely—managing what you have coming into the household. It starts with knowing what you're spending and dealing with what most people view as the horrible concept of budgeting. I've learned to actually enjoy budgeting on a monthly basis. Because needs change, the budget also needs to change. Budgeting can actually be a positive thing because it gives you permission to spend in areas that are a priority to you. Depending on how limited the income is, you may have to cut back in other areas to have room in the budget for those priority items. These could be things like a child's birthday that month, summer camp, or a trip.

Have a plan for every dollar that you make. This includes savings and giving. The most important first step is creating and maintaining your emergency fund. To start, you need to have $1,000 in an emergency fund. If you don't have this right now, saving it up is your first goal. An emergency fund needs to be in a savings account, not your checking account. It's also not a place that you're going to be tapping each month to pay your regular bills.

Make sure when you talk about money that you keep a positive attitude around your kids. Rather than say, "We can't afford to buy that or go on that vacation," talk with them about what their desires are and then spend time letting them research how much that "want" costs. If they are too young to do this on their own, then work on it as a family. Help them understand the cost, if there's a way to do it on a smaller budget, how much you all need to save, and how much time it will take in order to make that happen. If it's something that your child(ren) wants to buy at the store, often times their desire for that item will wane by the time they've saved for it. If they save for it and still want it, then it probably is something that they will cherish. If they earn money toward something they want, it will allow them to be better financial stewards because everything won't be handed to them. Also, when your children see you saving for things you want rather than putting them on credit, they won't have an entitlement mentality.

When You're in the Weeds

So, what if you are running at a deficit each month? I'm sure you've heard the definition of insanity: doing the same thing and expecting different results. You have to change the situation you're in. You either need to cut expenses or create more income. This could be finding a cheaper cell phone plan or cancelling cable—I grew up without cable and turned out just fine. Making meals based on what's on sale, and eating out less or not at all also helps.

I know as a busy single mom, it's much easier to swing by the drive through at the end of the day when you're exhausted rather than go home and cook, so making this switch is going to take some planning on your part so it's not 6 PM and you have no food to cook for dinner. I have found a few dozen crock pot meals that are easy to dump in before leaving the house in the morning or better yet make ahead on a weekend and freeze so I can grab it when I know my evening is going to be frenzied due to sports practices, meetings, etc.

Your other option is to make more money. Have you just settled for a J-O-B? Do you have a skill that could be paying you more? It's easy to get complacent. Are others in your position making more either at your company or elsewhere? Have you ever gotten a raise? Women tend to settle and don't ask for more or when offered a job they don't counter offer. I encourage you to do so. What's the worst that can happen? They say no and the choice is still yours.

Getting Out of Debt

Once you have created your budget, have gotten a handle on what your monthly expenses are, and are able to spend less than you make, you have to figure out what this extra money is going to do for you. It may have to go toward paying off debt. While this process may take major sacrifices and daily discipline, it will be so freeing once you're out of debt. How do you do this and is there any order to paying your debt off? Yes.

You may know the difference between secured and unsecured debt. Secured debt always has a lower interest rate because there is some kind of collateral attached to the debt. These are things like a home, car, or property.

Unsecured debt carries a much higher interest rate and many times can be variable. The obvious is credit card debt; however, more and more young people also have student loan debt. Student loans typically have a lower interest rate than credit cards and for the most part are fixed rates.

There are different methods to paying off credit card debt. Most experts and I agree that what is termed the Snowball Method works best. With this approach, you take the smallest balance (assuming you have multiple credit cards with balances) and apply any extra money towards that debt while paying just the minimums on all other credit cards. Once that credit card is paid off, apply the amount you were paying on that card and apply it to the next smallest card. Do this until they are all paid off.

The reason this method is successful is because of the mental psychology behind it. You are seeing progress as each one gets paid off, and because the first card is the smallest amount you will see results quicker than if you took for instance the card with the highest interest rate.

Speaking of interest rates, if you have made regular payments on your credit cards I would recommend calling each company and requesting a lower interest rate. Explain that you are trying to get your debts paid off and would appreciate any consideration they can give you by lowering your interest rate. Most companies will work with you and lower it a few percentage points. This too will help in the long run as you will be repaying less money.

When you get your credit card debt paid off, take that additional money and apply it to any auto or student loan payments you have. This whole process could take months or years, but the quicker you're able to get it paid off the better you're going to feel about your future and the quicker you can get on to more important tasks for your money.

~Amy Whitlach, Thrivent Financial, Amy.Whitlach@Thrivent.com

Chapter 5: Life Post-Divorce

Learn from your mistakes, then move on.

I grew up in a family where the parents ruled and had all the say—the children were not to speak up. If there were any issues, you had to sweep it under the rug. I realize now how much that attitude impacted me. Your childhood molds you; it establishes your belief system, values, and your map: how you view the world and handle life.

Now, don't misinterpret what I am saying and think you can blame your childhood experience (no matter how negative it may have been) for your current life status. You are 100% in control of your own mind, choices and behavior. I know plenty of people who didn't have the most ideal upbringing and are loving life and achieving their goals. It comes back to your mindset. Have you grown? Have you taken a difficult situation and learned from it? You can absolutely take a negative experience and turn it into something positive. Let your struggle be a catalyst for you.

When I was married, I hadn't grown enough to be able to improve my communication skills. It definitely is more challenging to have healthy communication when your partner is closed off to it. Looking back now, however, I should have insisted on more open communication, but I was much weaker back then. I tolerated a lot of things I shouldn't have. I take full responsibility in my part of our failed relationship. Did it suck getting divorced? Hell, yes. But I learned a lot from it.

> *There are going to be times when you feel like a total failure. Times when you don't want to make dinner, and you give your kids cereal for every meal of the day. Just know you're not alone, because at one point we all do it. You didn't fail, you fed your kids and you kept your sanity. That's all that matters! ~Jennifer*

Moving

Initially, my son and I stayed in the house for a few months. Then once my ex served me with papers, everything changed. We put the house up for sale, as I could not afford it on my own. To my surprise, it sold instantly. I was not prepared for that. It was a shock to my system and made it all real. I had to pack up the entire house all by myself with a young kid in tow. I had to clear out the two-car garage that we used for storage, as well as the shed with all our tools, grill, mower, etc. It was extremely time consuming and back breaking.

I had no other choice, so I decided to make the most of it and was able to sell a lot of items and make some money for myself. Looking back, I wish my realtor hadn't known the reason we were selling the house. I feel like she illegally told prospective buyers and presented us with lowball offers. At that point, however, I didn't have the energy to fight it. I was happy just to be getting by. Once the house sold, I obviously had to find a new place to live.

It was hard to move out of the home I had created, the home my son was born and raised in, the home we extensively remodeled to make our own. However, I realized that at the end of the day it wasn't really a "home." It was basically a structure with walls; it no longer had a strong foundation. As they say, home is where the heart is— it is comprised of the people and love in it. Home can be found anywhere as long as there is love.

I am a total school snob, so I knew I wanted to stay in my son's current district. I also was determined to keep him in the same school in the wake of the divorce to avoid too many changes at once. The tricky thing was my town was not a rental community; it was an upper middle-class beach community where many residents commuted into Manhattan for work. As you can imagine, the few rentals that existed were not cheap.

Always the optimist, I went to view a two-story colonial house way out of my price range in hopes of charming the owner. Boy, was I glad I took that chance! The owner happened to be a single dad, slightly older than me, who understood my situation. He even allowed my three dogs though he initially said no pets, and lowered the rent just so I could afford it. Thank you, God!

My philosophy is it is always worth asking. If you don't ask, then the answer will always be no. I am huge believer of telling the universe what you need and want. You have to be really specific so it knows what to bring to you. We wound up loving our rental; it was perfect for us. We had a lot of space and a huge yard.

When Your Divorce is Final

I know lots of women who shout out to the world when their divorce is final. Many go out and celebrate. I never felt that way; I never was happy about it. On the surface I may not appear it, but I am a really sensitive person. I feel things deeply and have to be careful about allowing my emotions to overcome me. My mind is always thinking; it is hard for me to shut it down. This is why I can be a workaholic at times. It redirects my thinking to something positive—creating my empire and having financial abundance so I can feel secure and safe.

Divorce takes that sense of security away from you—safety is ripped off like a Band-Aid. My life is not how I imagined it to be. I always wanted to have a big family, lots of kids, dogs running around, crazy holidays. That is why my friendships are extremely important to me. My friends are my chosen family whom I love fiercely. I have so much love to give and share.

Forgive your ex. ~Danielle

What's Your Story?

It's amazing how powerful your mind is. The stories you tell yourself can make you play it small and safe while preventing you from achieving new levels and dreams. When you have a fixed mindset, you believe you have a set level of abilities, intelligence, and talents. An example would be, "I'm not good in math." Conversely, in a growth mindset, you understand your talents and abilities can grow as a result of your efforts. Fixed mindset people are afraid of making mistakes and looking stupid. They will do anything they can to protect themselves from failure. This allows them to avoid failure in the short term, but prevents them from great success in the long run. It also often hinders their health and happiness.

I don't believe it is the smartest person who is the most successful. The happiest and most successful people are those who believe in themselves and are willing to learn, make mistakes, fail and keep retrying. You only truly fail when you don't try or give up too easily. Life is all about learning from your mistakes and growing.

Love Your Failures

I have failed countless times throughout my life, in business ventures and relationships. You know what? It's okay! It's more than okay. I have grown so much in my 42 years of life and I like the person I am now. I love evolving and navigating through this crazy thing called life. When there is something I am not good at, it challenges and inspires me to learn that specific skill set.

There is something to be said for being self-educated. I've had to do it a lot since my divorce, on personal and professional levels. Acquiring a new skill set is *such* a high for me. It gives me an incredible amount of confidence and happiness. I know I freaking rock and have no shame in shouting it out! I've worked hard to get to where I am.

A growth mindset allows you to overcome challenges, which is imperative since we all know how difficult life can be. If you are realizing you currently have a fixed mindset, I invite you to find a goal, say running a 5K race, and start small but make sure you take action daily until it becomes a habit. Start with walking for five minutes. The next day, up it to 10 minutes. As you increase your time, mix it up—five minutes of walking, five minutes of running. Before you know it, you will be a runner!

Daily Action

I always tell my training and coaching clients, "Baby steps!" Make sure you are taking some sort of action daily toward your dreams because life is all about the regular choices we make. Those small choices can make a huge difference in the long run because your daily actions will change the belief you have about yourself. Stay focused on each day as opposed to the end result. Do not let the results define you—it's more about the person you become while taking daily action, than about the results.

Love yourself enough to dedicate time each and every day for yourself. Show up for yourself and again, focus on the process and not just the outcome. Writing this book is the perfect example of this idea. I wrote the first draft myself. When I realized it needed to be longer and needed more content, I kind of froze. I doubted my abilities to get it done. Fortunately, being a coach myself, I 100% believe in *having* a coach. So, what did I do? I hired a writing coach/ghostwriter! I wrote the book myself, but she polished and edited it for me. She gave me weekly homework assignments which kept me on task. I needed that extra push, that accountability partner who ensured I did the daily things I needed to do to get this book written. A book isn't written in a day. You have to commit to it over the course of several months, writing a little at a time. That small amount of new material each day starts to add up.

Divorce Aftermath

I was sad about my divorce, but by the time we got to that point, I felt ready to move on. I didn't want to feel sad or lonely anymore. Being separated actually made me feel better because it gave me hope. Our divorce took a few years. I was in no rush for it to be finalized, because it was just a piece of paper to me. Our marriage was long over by the time it was officially over. However, when I got notice that we were finally legally separated, I did cry. It really hurt and all the emotions and feelings came rushing back.

The finality of it was a hard hit for me. I hate failing and I hated ripping our family apart. My biggest struggles were guilt, embarrassment and judgment. What would other people think of me? Even now, I am still like that, to a point. I think we all are on some level. We worry and care about what others think, even though what others think of us shouldn't be our concern. I remember getting the letter and just bawling my eyes out. It wasn't even so much that I missed my husband, it was more the failure and lost dreams...the broken family for my son. I now realize there is no one definition of family.

I struggle with my decision to move to Florida, to take my son away from his dad. It's an internal struggle that I still battle. Was I being ultra-selfish? Does he regret allowing us to move? Am I ruining their relationship? They do see each other and keep in touch; I never keep my son away from his dad. He has even started flying up to New York on his own to visit him. Still, I wonder if my son will resent me as he gets older and understands more. Will he want to move back to live with his dad when he is older? My son doesn't know any of the reasons for our divorce. I wonder what he will think of me. Will he judge me? He was young enough to not question our divorce; he barely remembers us living together as a family.

As for feeling vulnerable, I hate the stigma that comes with being a single mom. I hate the statistics with a vengeance. My son is brilliant. I don't foresee him being some dropout when he is older, yet society likes to make you believe that children of single moms are really bad off. I feel as if I need to prove them wrong, as well as prove it to myself to justify my decision.

I put so much effort, time, and energy in being there for my son. I just want the best for him. I want him to be happy and love his life—to not feel he missed out on things because he wasn't raised by a married couple. I feel fortunate that he had both of us when he was young, during his formative years. I worry about his teen years, when a boy needs a positive male role model. Will he have enough time with his dad? I want to raise my son to be a strong, confident male. At the same time, I want him to be caring and sensitive.

I think it can be harder for single moms to get a good job. Stereotypes still exist, for all types of people. Being a female, Latina, *and* a single mom definitely doesn't help at times. I want to be able to provide for my son. I want to feel strong and independent and self-sufficient. I want to teach Ethan to rely on himself. Even though life can get hard, I am teaching him he can get through anything.

Sisterhood Evolution

One of the ways I empower myself and my son is via entrepreneurship. Sisterhood Evolution, the online apparel store I co-founded, was born from the notion of women supporting women. I have been blessed to have an amazing network of women in my life. My friends are my chosen family. With that being said, I have realized that many women are lacking this sort of friendship and bond in their lives. It is imperative that women do not feel alone and isolated. We need to be there for one another.

Throughout my lifetime, people would always tell me how lucky I am to still be friends with people from my early childhood. I have this amazing ability to connect with women and form deep relationships with them. I have made and remained friends with people from school, college, work and clients of all different nationalities, religions and walks of life. Women feel comfortable around me. At the end of the day, we are all women and nothing can change that commonality.

One of my strengths and joys is introducing women to one another. I love seeing the new connections and support they give to each other. Life can be tough, so it is nice to have your girls to call upon. My goal is to have Sisterhood Evolution become a movement—something women want to become a part of. Unity and strength in numbers. No more competition or jealousy between women. Instead, lets stand bravely side by side and achieve tremendous things. We are a community. Together we can accomplish anything. Female loyalty. Solidarity. An army of women to back you up. Belief in one another. True friendship. Lifetime friendship. Empowering, celebrating, accepting one another. Freedom. Social change. A sense of belonging. Uplifting, slaying, loving. A special connection. Nonjudgmental, caring, understanding. Fun. Close ties.

To me, Sisterhood conveys emotions and feelings while Evolution represents development: Women growing and learning together...evolving. Becoming stronger, the person they are meant to be. Living life with purpose and meaning. Together, we can change the world, with the change beginning in us. Improving upon ourselves and the world.

I originally came up with the idea of Sisterhood of Single Moms since I run a Facebook page for single moms. I had my friend, who is a designer, come up with a design for a t-shirt I wanted to sell. As I was telling her my concept and dream, she fell in love with the whole idea. We decided to expand it to Sisterhood Evolution to include all women. That's when she asked me if she could partner up with me. Her specialty is web design, IT, and social media marketing; I would be the face of the company and marketer.

We have been friends for years and our boys are very close friends. The partnership made sense to both of us so we decided to create an online apparel store together. We have big visions for our company; we are not just about the apparel. We believe in personal development and growth and having a community of women who support one another on a personal and business level.

As for the selection of the clothes, we pick out various styles that will complement all the beautiful figures that women have, from petite to extra-large. We want women to feel comfortable and confident in their own skin. The attire will complement their bodies and feel good on them. We have trendy pieces, outfits, accessories and more, as well as classic items. We will have more affordable items, as well as some luxury pieces to satisfy the various palates of our customers.

Overthinking

While divorce certainly is an emotional roller coaster, the same is also true for being a single mom. Self-doubt, loneliness, isolation and depression can all come into play. Women tend to question their choices and place tremendous guilt on themselves for breaking up the family. Females completely overthink things. Our minds never stop. We are like a computer with a million tabs open all the time.

From the second I awake in the morning, information and feelings consume my mind. My mind races even when I'm trying to fall asleep at night. I have a notebook on my nightstand so I can write down my thoughts and my to-do list. Sometime I have to listen to sleep music or hypnotherapy to prevent my mind from racing. Lavender oil and my eye mask have become my best friends.

It's quite amazing how some men have the ability to simply shut off their minds. It seems to me that many men don't have intertwining highways of thoughts and feelings racing endlessly through their brains. I can't, as a woman, image having such a simple, guiltless way of thinking. I am jealous of men who can turn off the spigot. In my next lifetime, I may just have to come back as a man!

Women tend to focus on all the good times they had during their marriages, instead of remembering the reasons why they got divorced. We need to have a good support team and friends we can talk to and rely on when we're feeling low. I was fortunate to join a few Facebook private groups for single moms that really help. We offer advice and support to one another. It's nice to know you aren't alone.

The Weekends

When my ex-husband and I first separated, the hardest part for me was the weekends when I didn't have my son. I cried my eyes out each time his dad came to pick him up. I had never been away from my son like that and hated not knowing what he was doing without me. It was pure torture the first time my ex-husband had him around another woman and her family. It felt like a big ole slap in the face. Fortunately, I had a good friend who was firm, and told me as long as my son is safe and happy I need to learn to accept the situation. Sometimes you just need tough love from a friend.

When I changed my frame of mind and let go of control, I learned to appreciate my free weekends. I had time to run errands, pamper myself, and spend time with my mom and girlfriends. I tell moms new to these kid-free weekends to get a hobby or do volunteer work. Giving to others less fortunate than you tends to put things into perspective and takes the focus off of your situation. Giving is a full-circle gift, as the giver gets much joy and pleasure from the act of giving.

Social Media

After I separated from my ex-husband, it was amazing how many people approached me and revealed how unhappy they were in their marriages. It goes to show how little we really know about what's actually going on, behind those smiling vacation pictures on social media. I don't believe in Facebook anymore; I now call it Fakebook. Couples declare their love for one another on Facebook while secretly being miserable. It makes me laugh when I see stuff like that online. People who feel the need to make a big show of their relationships are usually the people who aren't happy with their marriage.

If you are truly happy in your relationship, you won't feel the need to post it on social media. Beautiful vacation and family photographs only show the happy times. Little does anyone know that a moment ago, the kids were having the biggest temper tantrum, or you and your spouse were just yelling at one another. No one posts the photos of the dog peeing on the rug, while one kid is throwing up, the other is swinging from a hanging light, and the husband is sitting on the couch laughing at sports bloopers.

You have to love Facebook for what it is. Facebook is a fake arena where people post only the best moments of their lives. Many people photoshop or filter their pictures to make them look perfect. While I like having photos as a memento, when I am truly in the moment and enjoying the company I am with, I am not necessarily thinking about taking a photo to upload instantly on Facebook or Instagram. Our society likes to show off, and Facebook is the perfect platform for it. Sadly, many people suffer from jealousy and depression as a result of believing that everyone else's life is better than theirs. Don't even get me started with the ridiculous drama that occurs on Facebook, too.

Stress less, play more.

People tend to compare their lives with others. Try to keep in mind that you are only seeing a glimpse of reality, and that comparison just makes you feel inadequate. Stay in your own lane. Do not worry about what others are doing. Instead, focus on gratitude. Choose to appreciate all the wonderful things in your life. What you focus on expands. I challenge you to write down three things you are grateful for on a daily basis. You will be amazed how your perspective changes.

If you're anything like me, you probably always mentally analyze every thought and action, and social media doesn't help. Single moms often always ask themselves, "Am I doing the right thing?" or "Am I with the right person?" Impressionable women see one version of people's fake lives on Facebook and strive for that kind of perfection, forgetting sometimes that it simply *does not exist*. Facebook should be in the same category as everything on television, produced or reality. None of it is real, yet people mold their lives around this false reality, this illusion. A woman may even leave her current situation because she wants the kind of relationship she sees on Facebook. But she will never find what she seeks, because what she *thinks* exists was really just a dream.

Married Men

It annoys me how creepy some married men act toward me. They totally cross the line and flirt, which is completely inappropriate and turns me off big time. I would *never* be with a man who could act like that.

Ladies, please don't be dumb and fall for their empty promises of leaving their wives. You are smarter than that. If a man is willing to cheat on his wife and ruin his family, what makes you think he wouldn't cheat on you? Have you ever heard the expression, "Once a cheater always a cheater?"

Judgment

I thoroughly dislike how judgmental and unsupportive people can be about divorce. They feel like you are being selfish and are hurting the kids. I disagree. Children are very perceptive. They see and know more than you think. You can feel the tension in the air of an unhappy household, even if the parents don't yell or disagree in front of the family. How is *that* healthy for kids? You are teaching them it's okay to be unhappy and to squash your feelings.

I have seen kids who acted out terribly while the parents were married, but once they divorced, the kids were much happier and their behavior improved. If you stay in an unhappy marriage, the kids suffer, especially if you are depressed. Don't fool yourself into believing that your negative situation won't affect your kids.

It takes a lot of courage to leave a toxic relationship. You need to show your children what a healthy relationship looks like. Do not believe it's better to stay in a bad situation for the sake of the kids. That is ridiculous. Children always know when there is tension or fighting. It can be extremely damaging to a child who has to listen in fear to their parent fight. This trauma leads to many issues as an adult.

I would much rather be single than show my child an unhappy marriage. In the end, only *you* can decide what is best for your family. You must learn to silence the critics and listen to your gut. The first year I was separated, I only told my closest friends because I was embarrassed and ashamed. Since then, I have learned to not care about what society thinks about me, or my lifestyle. This is *my* life to live, not theirs. If you are happy, then your children will be happy. In time, I realized just how many divorced couples there actually are. You might be surprised to see just how many single moms there are out there.

If you're feeling judged, I recommend limiting the amount of time you spend online. You will see countless articles about how to best parent your kids, stories about the damage that divorce inflicts on kids, etc. Don't take to heart what you read. People will form their own opinions, and those opinions will cause you to doubt yourself if you take them too seriously. An opinion is like a belly button, everyone has one. Just do the best you can, and don't worry about what anyone else thinks or says to you.

We place enough guilt on ourselves. We don't need to receive more stress from articles and other people. I've learned the people shouting advice often are the people that know the least. Unfortunately, fellow mothers can be the worst critics, and are often guilty of being judgmental. Often times, those judging are not even in the same position as you. They have no idea of everything you are going through and just how strong you really are. Stay clear of people who think they know it all. I do not know it all and I am in no way trying to tell you what to do. The purpose of this book it to let you know that you are not alone in this journey and to offer advice, but it is entirely up to you to choose how you will live your life. You must stand by your principles and feel proud of all you have accomplished.

Just because you are having a bad day, it doesn't mean you are a bad mom.

In-Laws

Many times, after a divorce, your in-laws will cut ties with you. Work hard, if you can, to make sure your ex-husband still has your kids interact with these family members. The divorce shouldn't change the relationship they have together. If your in-laws remain in your life, and the relationship is not strained or broken through the divorce, consider yourself fortunate because that's the best possible situation. Kids benefit from having family and people who love them as a constant part of their life. Never try to isolate your kids from your exes' family.

Guilt

Let's list all the things single moms feel guilty about:

- Taking away the experience of family life
- Working too much
- Missing out on experiences with their children
- Dating
- Change in income level and lifestyle
- The emotional wellbeing of our children

It goes on and on...you get the point. Relax, Mama—your child has made it this far. Guilt in small doses is okay, but you can't allow it to consume you and control your life.

Too much guilt can cause you to isolate yourself, lose yourself, and make poor decisions. If you are feeling overwhelmed with guilt, be sure to seek out professional help so you don't have to face it alone. Don't feel guilty about needing help, either. Be kind to yourself and forgive yourself if you make mistakes. We have all made mistakes at one point or another. No one is perfect. Some people are just better at hiding personal imperfections. Making mistakes is how you grow. If you never make mistakes, then you are never challenging yourself to grow as a person. Never fear self-growth or improvement, even if the process is painful.

You Know You're a Single Mom When...

- Going to the store alone feels like a vacation.
- Taking long, hot baths is a luxury.
- You rarely get to pee in private.
- You are happy when it's bedtime.
- You can do several things at once, one-handed.
- You constantly doubt yourself.
- You hold 10 packages in your hand while your kid holds one little measly thing.
- You have mastered sleeping on the edge of a bed without falling off.
- You constantly battle between going to bed early or staying up to do adult things.
- Your to-do list is never-ending.
- You love your kids one minute and then you are ready to sell them the next minute.

- You no longer buy stuff for yourself.
- You are lucky if you brushed your hair today.
- You often wonder how you will survive.
- You decide hangovers aren't worth it.
- You have ninja-like hearing.
- You realize you have watched 30 minutes of *Dora the Explorer* even though your kids have been in bed the last half-hour.
- You have fallen asleep putting your kids to bed.
- The scariest one—you sound like your mother!
- You want to cry but you smile instead.
- Pulling an all-nighter has a whole new meaning.
- You are dead tired during the day but have insomnia at night.
- You wonder if you will be single forever.
- You pulled the Santa card.
- You forgot to move that damn elf!

Chapter 6: Friendship

You are beautiful.

One thing I love about my girlfriends is that we are not perfect, not do we pretend to be. We don't sugar coat things with one another. Our modus operandi is brutal honesty but in a loving manner. Tough love. We laugh at one another and we also support and empower one another.

I don't resonate or click with those "perfect" sort of moms out there, the ones who are super prissy and try to give off the impression that they are perfectly poised. My girlfriends can admit to one another that sometimes our kids annoy the crap out of us, or that sometimes they really can't stand their spouse or significant other. We don't pretend to have it all together.

I've been told I sometimes give off the impression that I live this amazing life, that I am perfect and that people can't relate to me. I honestly didn't realize I gave off that impression. I tend to be a private person and only really open up to my closest friends. On social media, people only see the surface level Andrea. They have no idea about all my struggles.

One weekend I was in Miami, stayed at Lowes Hotel, and partied at Fontainebleau. I had this really lavish weekend and yes, I posted a pic on Facebook. The thing to understand about it, however, is this is *totally* not my norm. Prior to that experience, I hadn't had a weekend like that in over two years. Most people, myself included sometimes, just post the good stuff.

I am just like every other person out there. I wish I had a flatter stomach; I wish my hips were smaller. The scrutiny you get when you are a Personal Trainer and Health Coach is huge. People expect you to be perfect, to eat clean 100% of the time. I love chocolate cake and French fries just as much as the next person.

Lean on Your Friends

Like I said earlier, I wish there was more support for single moms—even support from one another. Less judgment. Many people are critical of divorced people. That is what makes me feel vulnerable and sad.

I am truly thankful for my friends. Someone special taught me this toast: *Here is to friends that become family and family that remains friends.* I can't stress enough the importance of having a good support system and people who will be there for you during your situation. The process of separation and divorce truly is an emotional roller coaster ride. Until you've been through it, you can't really understand the depths of it, what it does to your psyche. It shakes you to the core and can bring you to dark places. Many people hit rock bottom. The wonderful thing is, you can pull yourself back up and become stronger in the process. Have that growth mindset and learn from your mistakes.

Married Friends, Single Mom

I love all my friends, but sometimes my married friends drive me nuts. They complain when their husbands work late, or go out of town for work, and say they feel like a single mom. Um, no, not even close. At least you have a husband who is bringing home the bacon. Or they get upset when their husbands get their kids all riled up at night. Um, how about being happy your kids have their father present and involved in their daily lives? If married moms get sick, they have their husbands as backup. When a single mom gets sick life still goes on. I also love it when they complain about having to wait around for a service person to arrive. I would love to have the money to hire people to do jobs for me, and the time to sit around and wait. It's hard to be around married couples when you are going through a divorce. I think that is why so many single people tend to connect and hang out. We understand what we are going through.

I'm not going to lie, I get jealous when I see dads bringing their kids to the school bus, or attending school functions. I never had that with my ex-husband. It must be so nice to have someone who is an active partner in raising the children. I find it ironic that all I really wanted in life was to be married with a few children, yet I still don't have that at age 42. I sometimes wonder what my life would have been like had I married someone else, or if I had fought harder for what I wanted in my marriage. However, I would never actually change it, because then I wouldn't have my son whom I love with all my heart. I tell myself that God knows what He is doing and only He knows what the future holds for me. I have learned to accept my life for what it is at the moment and to trust my journey.

I get envious of my friends who are able to stay home all day with their kids, and the ones who don't work even though their kids are in school all day. They get to play on social media and meet their friends for breakfast and lunch. Maybe having feelings like these makes me a bad friend. I have an incredible amount of stress in my life, so I simply don't have the time or energy to worry about trivial things anymore. Being a single mom makes you open up your eyes and put things into perspective. There is no time for drama.

It's difficult not to compare yourself, or your situation, with anyone else's, but motherhood is a personal journey and no two people have the same experience. Each child and situation is unique. Each mother is different. Single moms will face more hardships than a mom that isn't single, but that's okay, excelling through dire times will make you and your family unit stronger. While all mothers sacrifice for their children, single moms tend to over sacrifice to make up for the guilt of divorce. Just remember, while it may seem as if everyone else has their act together, you really have no idea what is happening behind closed doors. People put on their best game face and act as if their lives are perfect, when in reality they have their own set of issues to deal with.

Loneliness

Being a single mom can be extremely lonely. Sometimes when I stop and think, it dawns on me just how utterly and completely alone I am. At the end of the day, I have my son and my mom, and my mom won't be around forever. I notice the feeling of lonesomeness the most around the holidays. You see large family gatherings, but you are all alone. I don't have many people to buy presents for but I can choose to be happy I don't have to spend a lot of money.

It's very easy to jump on the pity train. Have your sad moments and bad days, but make sure you don't stay there. You have to be strong for your children. You must make the most of the life you were given. Stay positive and see all the beauty that life offers. Be brave and live your life the way you choose. Go after your dreams. You are in control of your destiny, no one else. Let go of the blame, learn from your lessons, and keep moving forward. Don't look backward, you aren't going there. Enjoy the journey and the crazy ride. I have faith you will persevere. Believe in yourself and your abilities.

Find Your Single Mom Tribe

Single moms must stick together. I do recommend finding other single moms, because your married friends just won't get it. I have learned over the years that people only know what they know and you can't fault them for that. Unless you have experienced divorce or single motherhood firsthand, you can't fully comprehend it. My only issue with some single mom groups is the same caution I mentioned previously regarding support groups in general: some divorced women are very bitter and can't let go of the anger. Don't let yourself fall into that trap. You must not feel sorry for yourself. Give yourself time to be sad and grieve, then move on. Surround yourself with positive, uplifting people who will motivate you to do your best.

Perhaps younger single moms should join forces with an older single mom. This way they can give some pointers and advice. They have been through the battlefield and can help. They can also give us hope that there is life post-divorce. Many people find the love of their lives after their first marriage. It is important to stay hopeful and positive.

Most people can agree that making new friends as an adult isn't particularly easy, but it is possible. Meet other great people in your area by participating in meetup.com groups, Facebook groups, neighborhood organizations and other local groups. The single moms Facebook group that I run can be found by searching for "Sisterhood of Single Moms" on Facebook. We'd love to have you join us!

Losing Friendships

Divorce will reveal to you who your true friends are. Some people might side with your ex-husband. Others might stop including you in social events since you aren't part of a couple. Some might judge you. Friends come into your life for a reason, it could be just for a season or to teach you a lesson. Try not to take things personally. People change and grow. Each stage of your life brings you different gifts. Most of my best friends now are single moms who understand and get me. It's beneficial for our kids to see they aren't the only ones with divorced parents. It normalizes things for them. They can relate to one another.

It's interesting that post-divorce some of my married friends no longer reached out to me. I think some insecure women feel threatened by the thought of a single woman around her husband, which is completely ridiculous. I would never go after a friend's husband, nor would I ever break up a marriage. If you truly know me, that thought would never cross your mind. Plus, why would I be with a man who would cheat on his own wife? I also find many husbands do not like their wives going out with their single friends, especially if their marriage is not solid.

Many married men are insecure enough to harbor the mistaken notion that a single woman will poison their wives in some way and influence them to consider ending their own marriage. Men know that women talk about relationships. If the couple is having marital issues, they worry their wives will see how happy the single friend is and might consider divorce for themselves. The mere thought of a single friend planting a seed in their wife's mind can be exceptionally threatening to a husband. Many couples like to stay in their safe bubble, and pretend everything is perfect. They do not want external influences ruining their façade.

Chapter 7: The Perks

You are a badass mom. You are enough.

There are many pros of being a single mom. You can be your own superhero! I would much rather be single than suffer in a bad marriage. Since I know I'm the one who has to handle the entire workload, I no longer need to fight a partner about doing certain chores or tasks. There's no more nagging, no more resentment, no more carrying around anger toward another person. Being single has taught me to be very efficient with my time.

Another pro is there is no one here to undermine my authority. What I say goes. I'm the boss. I no longer have to bicker or negotiate with a person who has a different parenting style than me. I get to raise my son the way I want to. Unilateral choices, baby! No more drama.

Another big perk is I don't have to share a closet with anyone! Come on ladies, how sweet is that? You can live the way you like to live, whether it's a as a neat freak or a mess. No one is there to complain if you want to eat in bed, let the dog sleep with you, watch chick flicks, or keep the heat on high. We can also break the rules and do whatever we want. Pizza for breakfast. Why not? Skip a family function. Go right ahead.

I also love having the bed to myself. I don't have to listen to a man snoring next to me, or fight for covers at night. The National Sleep Foundation reported that sleeping two to a bed could cause you to lose 49 minutes of sleep per night. That adds up!

When my son is asleep, it's finally me time. I don't have to worry about making time for a man and making him happy. I can focus on me and what I want to do. I now have time to talk with my besties on the phone or take a hot, relaxing bath. Girl time is extremely important to me and I can hit the gym without feeling guilty about it. Being single motivates you to look and feel your best.

Let's not forget how hot and steamy new relationships can be. Often when you are married for many years, you get in a sexual rut. Sex can become routine and boring. New divorcees tend to be excited to meet new people and experiment. Being single allows you to pick and choose who you want to be with. You get to enjoy new lovers and maybe try things you didn't while you were married. I think this is particularly true for men, as many don't think of their wives in the same way they would a single woman, especially if she is the mother of their child.

You're in Charge!

Since I want the best for my son, he inspires me to be successful in my career and life. I'm not relying on a man for my financial security and I don't allow a man to control me with his money. I know way too many wives who live like that. They receive an allowance from their spouse and have to ask for more money like a child. *I* control my finances, and how I spend my money.

Successfully navigating through parenthood is a boost to your confidence and self-esteem. You're in control of your destiny. It's entirely up to you to rock your life.

Be a terrific role model for your children—they will emulate your healthy behaviors. Show them you can be independent and don't need a man to make you happy or to survive. Most children of single moms learn to be more independent, responsible and self-sufficient. These are great life skills. My son and I are a team.

One pro for kids of single moms is they get all your attention since you aren't splitting it with a spouse. You have more bonding time together. It's also good for children to see life isn't always perfect. They are better prepared to face the challenges of the real world if they don't live in a bubble. Being too sheltered hinders one's ability to survive life's struggles.

Regardless of how challenging motherhood may be, I never ever regret having my son. He is the most important person in the world to me, with my mom right beside him. My son has given me intense joy and happiness. He has given me insight about life and about myself. Having a child teaches you sacrifice and to not be selfish. It truly amazes me how much you can love your child. I will never forget the moment I met him and he was placed on my chest. For me, nothing in life is better than my son. I would feel incomplete without him. Although my life is limited for now while he is young, I know it is a temporary thing and completely worth it.

Independence

Another positive of being a single mom is that the situation forced me to learn countless new things, and taught me not to rely on a man. I am now a lot stronger and more confident than before I was married. I no longer freak out when I see bugs, for example. Most of the time, I take the bugs and insects outside to be free instead of killing them.

I can set up my son's various video game systems, which was no small feat for me to learn. I am more car and tech savvy. Even my navigational skills have improved. Taking out the garbage and doing the yardwork have become normal chores for me now.

Being independent is a wonderful feeling. If you have female children, this is great for them to see. In the future, I would love to start a women-run organization that teaches other women how to live on their own, how to use tools, how to fix things around the house, how to work on cars, etc. Hitting rock bottom and knowing you have someone relying on you is a great motivator. Many successful people started at the bottom and rose up out of desperation. If you hit the bottom, you can only go up from there.

The New Me

Today, I really *know* myself—my weaknesses and my strengths. Now, in my relationships, whether platonic or romantic, I stand up for myself. I express myself without fear of being judged or of the other person getting mad. Wait...let me take that back a bit. I try to do it. It takes a lot of effort for me to do this, as a result of a lifetime of not being a good communicator. It's outside of my comfort zone, but I do it because I know the importance and significance of open and honest communication.

I've done a lot of growing up since my divorce—and gained a hell of a lot of self-awareness and personal development. I can proudly say I am a personal development nerd and guru. I learned about fixed versus growth mindset while in a real estate training week-long workshop, of all places. That is when I realized my ex had a fixed mindset and I had a growth mindset.

See the Lighter Side

If you want to keep your sanity as a single mother, it's imperative that you learn not to take life too seriously. Let go of the idea of perfection because that word doesn't exist and it's not real. Nothing in life is perfect and nobody is perfect. Try not to freak out about every spill or mess. Take a deep breath if you feel yourself about to lose it or remove yourself from the situation by giving yourself a time-out. Words can hurt your children so be careful about what you say out of anger or stress. Physically hurting anyone is never acceptable, especially an innocent child. Physical violence doesn't make children respect you. It just causes them to fear you (and possibly hate you).

Your children must know that you love them unconditionally. Make time every day for quality time with them. Be sure to provide stability and consistency. Your children will benefit from positive discipline and expectations. Act like their parent instead of their friend.

Moms are great at doubting their parenting skills and abilities. Relax. Your kids are doing just fine. You don't need to be a perfect mom. Surround yourself with other mothers of young kids so you can learn from each other and inspire one another. All you can do is try your best and love your children. It's tough always being the one who has to make the decisions. Trust your judgment and that everything will work out in the end.

Finding Acceptance

Now *that* is a hard thing for moms to do. Your current life may not be what you had in mind for yourself. That's okay. Your current situation isn't your end-all. Your future is what you make of it, and it's never too late to start over. Have a new life, a new relationship, a new family, a new career. There is no cookie-cutter definition of family. Family can include your friends, partners, co-workers, church members, and more.

Honestly, most of your married friends are jealous and living through you. They hang on your every word about your dates and wish they could have that feeling that comes with a new relationship, so don't get caught up in self-pity. No matter how difficult your life may be, others have it much worse. Self-love and acceptance are two great gifts you can give to yourself. Just enjoy being in the present moment. Enjoy the journey and the path you are on. Remind yourself that you are not perfect, but you are perfect the way you are.

On the next page, you'll read a short letter from my son. I asked him to write something for me, from the heart, for my book. I was interested in seeing how he felt, and the things he wrote validated my efforts and choices. My heart is full. I can't recommend this exercise enough!

Letter from My Son Ethan, 11

To Mom,

I feel loved by you, and like I am the most important person in the world to you, which I am. I'm definitely happy, living the best life I could possibly live. I don't know what I would do without you. You are always the class mom, you are always being a chaperone on field trips, and you are always helping with in-school things.

I have the things I want and need, and I usually have money from my dog sitting business that you help a little bit on. You always have so much work to do, and you're always doing things for me. You even chose a job just so you can work at home and spend more time with me. You're always making me happy by getting things for me, getting me involved with all kinds of stuff and keeping me active, and helping me whenever I need help with all kinds of stuff.

Love, Ethan

Chapter 8: Dating

Find your worth within yourself,
then find a man worthy of you.

Let's discuss dating. Are you ready for this? It is normal to feel scared and hesitant at first, but remember, growth only occurs when you stretch yourself and go out of your comfort zone. Dating has been an interesting experience for me. Five years post-divorce, and I am still trying to figure out the dating world and men. They most certainly are different creatures than us! I am usually the one that ends a relationship. I know what traits and behaviors I am willing to tolerate and those that I won't. Not only do I have to make sure a man is good for me, but he also has to be a great role model for my son.

I am picky and have high standards, and I'm good with that. At this point of my life, I am not settling, although I do know no one is perfect, nor am I. I keep very busy with my family and friends, so I don't need a man in my life. However, it would be nice to have someone by my side to share it all. I have been hurt and disappointed by a few guys, which makes me put a wall up.

People show you who they are right up front—you just need to listen and not push away or ignore the red flags. Often, what ends a relationship is a problem that you could have seen the first few months of dating if you were open to seeing the signs.

I will date for a while and then get discouraged. I take a break from dating for a few months, and then when I am feeling recharged I put myself out there again. Many of my single female friends feel the same way as me. They get discouraged and disgusted and take a break for a while, too. Still, exposing myself to new experiences and settings will help open up my world. You just never know where and how you will meet your true love.

I'm not single anymore, but I was for the first five years of my son's life. I feel this needs to be said, especially to the younger single moms: Focus on your kid, not on finding a man. Your child deserves your undivided attention until a man comes along who wants to be there for both/all of you.
~Carly

Love Languages

I learned about the 5 Love Languages, a concept from a book of the same name by Gary Chapman, through my coaching certification program. You can use the love languages to improve upon your relationships. It is powerful knowing what you need and enjoy in a relationship. Then you can share it with your partner so he can provide it, and vice-versa. I took the complimentary online quiz and was not surprised by my results. My highest score was physical touch, which also includes physical presence and accessibility. I've realized I can't be with a guy who isn't a good texter, LOL. Tied in second place were Acts of Service and Quality Time. Some people may call it needy, but I enjoy actually *seeing* the person I am supposedly dating.

I've always had a lot on my plate, so it is so nice for me when someone helps me and makes my life a little bit easier. I'd love to find a man who can complement my lifestyle. A good way to test the health of a relationship is to examine if your needs are being met by the other person. If not, *next*. I am officially putting it out to the universe, what I want and need in a man.

The Journey

It makes life much easier if you accept where you are in the current moment. I don't need to have my entire future planned out. The unknown is okay. I am exactly where I am meant to be on this journey called life. All my past experiences and relationships have put me the exact path I am meant to be on. Life is about the journey and who you become along the way. Learn what you can from past relationships and move forward. When you meet the right one for you, you will understand why the other ones didn't work out. Just like the song "Unanswered Prayers" by Garth Brooks. I know when I meet Mr. Right, it will feel right and will be effortless.

You should never have to chase a man when dating. When a guy is really into a girl, he will find the time to make her a priority. He will see her, write her and make her feel like the queen she is. No excuses. Actions speak louder than words.

Stand up for yourself. Have difficult conversation so you can communicate your needs. The sooner you express yourself, the sooner you will find out if your partner can fulfill your expectations. Say *no* to being treated like a maybe or an option. If he goes from hot to cold, then go to the next faucet.

Heal yourself so you don't make a mistake and pick a man who is convenient and not worthy. ~Sarah

You Deserve the Best

Don't try to change a person—that must come from within themselves. My advice is to live your own life, do your own thing, and be protective of who you spend your time with. Stay busy with your own life and dedicate zero time to games.

Don't waste your time with relationships that aren't going anywhere. Great guys do exist, you just have to ditch the wrong ones so you can be open to meeting the good ones. Sometimes, to begin a new story, you have to let the old one end. The longer we chase the wrong person, the less time you will have for the right person. Sometimes you can meet the right person at the wrong time.

You absolutely deserve the best. Don't settle for average or good enough. Ending relationships can be difficult and sad, and that is alright. Take the time to mourn and then let it go. Don't stalk your ex, either! You don't check on the garbage you threw out, do you? Somewhere out there is a man who is searching for you, who will appreciate you for who you are.

One difficult lesson I learned from direct experience is this: If a person hasn't dealt with their past demons and issues, they will not be able to have a healthy relationship, no matter how much they might care for you. I tend to be a "saver." I love helping others, but I have learned that people have to help themselves. Their desire to change has to come from within. So, be careful with your energy. If you give too much without receiving, it can do much damage to your soul and psyche. Know when to walk away to protect yourself.

Slow Down

I never recommend dating immediately after your separation, though many people do it as a way to get over their ex-husband and through the divorce. It's natural to want to feel desired and loved, so it makes sense that after being in a miserable situation you would run to the next person who shows any sort of attention. What usually occurs as a result from a quick rebound, however, is just another failed relationship.

Take time to be alone, learn about yourself, and analyze your marriage and what went wrong. Why did your marriage end? How did you contribute to it? What did you do right and wrong during your marriage? Ask these sorts of questions to make sure you don't keep making the same mistakes in each relationship you are in. Otherwise, you will never be truly happy and have a healthy relationship. Unless you are honest with yourself, you will continue to bring those negative habits to each new relationship. You must love yourself, believe in yourself, know yourself and your desires before you are truly ready to be in a flourishing relationship. Not doing the inner work is the reason why some people are on marriage number three or even four.

Knowing what you want in your next mate is extremely critical in finding the right partner. It's also about the right timing. Are you both in the right place of your life? Do you want the same things, share the same dreams? No matter how much chemistry you might have together, it won't work out unless you are on the same page. Do not be afraid to give up the good for the great. Never undervalue yourself.

I also tell women not to date a man who is recently separated. There are stages to the divorce process. If you are ready to find your soulmate, the man who is recently separated will not be ready for love. Most people want, and need, to play the field, experiment, and see what is out there. They need time for self-exploration. You don't want to be that rebound woman. Nothing good will come out of it, I promise you. You most likely won't stay with the first few men out of your marriage, either. It goes both ways. If you don't want to go through another divorce, take your time with dating. Don't rush to get too serious with anyone. Have standards and know what traits you are looking for in a man.

High Standards

Do not stay in a relationship you wouldn't want your daughter to be in. Do not waste your time and energy on men who are not emotionally available or ready for you. I see too many women hang on to a relationship that is not going anywhere for far too long. Your time and energy are precious; don't waste them on someone who won't give them back to you. You are only setting yourself up for hurt and disappointment. Maintaining standards on how you're willing to be treated is the greatest natural filter for getting rid of the wrong people in love. Do not stay in a relationship in hopes of changing the guy.

As a woman, you deserve to feel love and appreciation from a romantic relationship. As a mother, you must model what a healthy relationship encompasses and looks like. I suggest taking your time and listening to your gut. Be open to meeting other people, but pay attention to red flags and approach with caution. Be selective in who you decide to invest your time and emotions. It takes time to get to know people and see their true colors.

Don't be afraid to be alone. Riding solo is much better than settling on a future disappointment. Being single and happy is better than being taken and miserable. You most certainly don't want to divorce again. You mustn't rely on anyone else for your sense of self-worth or happiness. Once you learn to love yourself, it is much easier for someone else to love you. Remember that not everyone who is single is lonely, and not everyone who is taken is in love.
One thing we can all agree on is dating post-marriage is tough. Each situation comes with its own set of issues. Younger men might not be ready to settle down, older men might be too set in their ways. Divorced dads are hard to schedule and meet up with and may have a crazy ex-wife. Blending two families together can be really tough. Be sure to not settle for a one-sided relationship. Whatever you do, don't settle out of desperation. You don't need a man to be happy or complete, and neither do your children.

Dating Today

Dating now is completely different than it was 20 years ago. Dating before the internet seemed much simpler and more authentic. The introduction of online dating and dating apps have entirely changed the dating scene. Sadly, it seems as though many men are just interested in playing the field and sleeping around. Many men no longer court woman. Dating and romance often seem like a thing of the past. Make sure you take the time to get to know the man you are dating before getting physically intimate with them. You are better than a quick hookup. Don't lower your standards just because some insecure women do. One of the best ways to meet someone is organically, either on your own, through a friend, or through a local event group.

You must use caution when using online dating sites. Anyone can lie and make up whatever they want. However, I must admit that thousands of people have met their spouses online, so there is hope still for online dating. People can put up a façade even when dating in person. Dating apps can be superficial. It's basically window shopping. Something might look good on the mirror but you won't know how it will fit until you try it on.

I have some dating tips to offer:

- Don't give out your personal phone number or information right away.
- Meet in a public location.
- Be sure you know who you are communicating with and they are not crazy.
- You can get a free Google voice number.
- Listen to red flags and your intuition. If something doesn't feel right, trust your gut.
- Use the block function whenever necessary.
- Prior to going on a date, make sure a friend knows all the details of the date and contact information of your date.
- Sometimes you have to be brutally honest in order for a man to realize you are not interested in pursuing a relationship with them.

- The more you try to sugarcoat things, the more difficult it is to end things.
- Don't rush into dating.
- Take your time and make sure you have recovered from your divorce.
- Give yourself time to heal and learn to be on your own.

It's empowering to be independent. This helps prevent you from jumping from one bad relationship to the next. At the same time, try not to wait too long to date again. The longer you wait, you will become more set in your ways and it will be difficult to allow a man to enter your world.

I know you are used to being in a monogamous relationship from your marriage, but this is when you should be casting a large net and date around. This allows you to compare and contrast the various attributes and characteristics of men. You want to find a man who is most compatible for you and your situation. Don't ever assume you are in a monogamous relationship. Nowadays men talk to several women at once. Men also ghost you. You can be chatting for a while thinking things are going well, then suddenly, they disappear for no apparent reason. I have zero patience for that. If I'm writing to someone for a few days and then suddenly don't hear from them for a while, I will block and disconnect with them. Next!

Many of us have tried online dating sites and dating apps. Here are some typical things you come across over and over again with these dating tools:

- Penis pictures
- Foot fetishes
- Men looking for threesomes
- Married men
- Men wanting to save you
- Young inexperienced men looking for cougars
- Men wanting sex but no relationship
- Crazy men
- Controlling men
- Men looking to get hitched immediately
- Men who will not stop trying to communicate with you, even after you try to end things

Ahh, the joys of dating. NOT! I recommend taking your time before you jump into bed with a suitor too quickly because you might become emotionally attached even if he isn't right for you. Women tend to associate sex with love, while men can separate the two. Sex involves deeper personal emotions for a woman.

Don't rush to introduce your kids to your new boyfriend or it can lead to disaster for everyone involved. Make sure the relationship is serious and you are both on the same page about your future. Do be brave and stay positive. It only takes one to be your Mr. Right.

Do know what it is you hope to find. Are you looking to have fun or to meet your future spouse? Put yourself out there. Meet other singles. Try to have fun with it and not take it too seriously. When you least expect it, the right one will come along. Maybe you will meet your future husband at your kids' soccer game, you never know. You are worthy of love. Rejoice in your sexuality and don't worry about what others might think. That isn't your concern.

The One for Me

As for me, I am still searching for the one. It's hard because I find men with different qualities. Sometimes I wish I could custom create my own man—take all the best qualities from each one I've met to make the perfect man! Build-a-Bear exists for children; I'd like to create a Build-a-Man for adults. All kidding aside, nice men do exist. You might have to search longer to find them, but they are out there. You know the expression, you have to kiss a lot of toads before you meet your prince. Remain patient and positive that the right one will come along. God knows what he is doing. Have trust in Him.

I find it easy to find men to go out and have fun with, but that isn't enough for me. I also want a family man. To find a family man who also wants to go out and have fun with me would be the ultimate package. It's not healthy to make your entire life revolve around your kids. That's part of the reason many kids have a sense of entitlement and why many marriages fail. People lose themselves in being a parent. When one spouse puts all their attention on the kids, it forces them to neglect their spouse. Typically, it is the wife that is guilty of this; however, I have seen men fall trap to it too. I am not sure if women do this because we carry the child in us for nine months and have a special bond as a result. Regardless of the reason, this is not fair to your life partner.

You need a healthy balance. Don't forget that children are a result of the love that originated from husband and wife. One day your children will be all grown up and leave you. If you've made your entire life about them, what will you have in common with your spouse? Many couples become more like roommates than lovers. My parents went on weekly date nights and they were a positive example of what a healthy, loving marriage should be. I truly aspire to find what they had together. You should be a living example of what a healthy relationship looks like.

I find it funny when people ask me why I'm still single. They think they are complimenting me by saying I am pretty and that I could easily be swept up by a man. What they are forgetting is the fact that it's not only about a man wanting *me*, it is also requires me wanting the same man in return. Any relationship requires effort, commitment, communication and patience.

I'm not desperate, nor am I one of those people who must have a man in my life. I would, of course, love to have a partner, but I'm not going to rush into anything, settle, or make a mistake. For me, I need to have a connection and chemistry. I have tried dating men that I didn't necessarily find attractive but who were nice, in hopes that their personality would win me over. However, that didn't work for me. I try not to think of myself as a shallow person, but I definitely need to be physically attracted to the person for it to work out. Otherwise, I just see the person as a friend. I also have never been able to transition from seeing a male friend as anything more than just a friend.

One of my biggest challenges has been that I am friendly to everyone. In turn, many men misinterpret that as me being interested in them when I'm not. It's frustrating as a woman when men are just nice to you because they would like to have a chance to be with you. I really wish it were easier to have platonic relationships with the opposite sex. It seems like women can do it but men always want more.

You're a Catch, Single Mama!

There is stigma to dating single moms, which is ridiculous. We are not full of issues, nor do we come with emotional baggage. We are super strong, mature and independent. We clearly communicate our needs and wants. We don't need a man; we would like one. We are adaptable and realistic. We know life isn't perfect, which means we don't expect a man to be. We already have a child, so we don't feel pressured by our internal clock ticking. We aren't needy nor do we play games.

We are in the prime of our lives—sexually, that is. Many moms have come out of sexually unsatisfying marriages and are ready to try new things. We are selfless and put other's needs before ours. We make sacrifices all the time and will do the same for our man. It is a delicate balancing act trying to be a good mother and girlfriend, so we are patient and understanding. We are very caring and nurturing. We are smart and know how to survive. We can handle anything that comes our way. Most moms aren't materialistic; we care more about experiences.

Many single moms wonder if men will want to date a woman with kids, or will they see them as baggage. You should run from a man who doesn't appreciate the life you have to offer, regardless of how much you might like him. You and your kids come as a package deal. Finding the time to date, especially if you have your children all of the time, can be extremely difficult. I suggest making friends with another single mom and taking turns watching each other's kids so you don't have to pay for a sitter. I personally don't want to pay for a sitter unless I absolutely have to or I know it will be worth the money.

When to Introduce Your Children

One of the most common questions divorced women face is when is the appropriate time to introduce a new romantic partner to their children. The answer is complicated. If you do it too soon, you're liable to confuse your children if the relationship doesn't work out. If you wait too long, you run the risk of finding out that your partner isn't great with children. Everyone has their own opinion.

I recommend taking your time dating post-divorce and not introducing your new love to your kids if you are dating casually. Six months is a good time frame to see if the relationship is getting serious. I will never have a revolving door, shuffling men in and out of my house, which is also my son's house. Your children need stability, and the last thing you need to do is add confusion or hurt to the situation.

Some children will quickly become attached to your new partner, especially if their dad is not involved or in the picture. The last thing you need is your child getting attached to a man you are not serious about. Kids aren't stupid. They won't believe this new man is just a friend. I don't think you should wait too long (as in, a year) to introduce your children to your romantic interest because you want to see for yourself how they interact and get along.

> *Don't introduce every boyfriend to your kids. Wait for*
> *someone you know is going to be around for a while.*
> *~Virginia*

You have to give it time, but then you must decide what you will do if they don't get along. Kids can wreak havoc on a relationship if they don't like the man. Depending on the relationship you have with your child's father, the two of you may decide on the appropriate timeframe to introduce the kids to your significant others. Overall, the quality of the relationship is more important than the quantity of time you are together.

The first introduction should be brief, casual and preferably in a group setting. You might want to have other adult friends there as well. This helps alleviate pressure and is non-threatening. Your children will need time to get used to a new situation, so proceed slowly. Initially, I would continue doing group settings to help ease into the situation, at a neutral location (as opposed to at the child's house).

Another important consideration when introducing your kids to your new partner is the age of your child. Younger children (under the age of 10) may feel confused, angry or sad about your new relationship. Little boys tend to be possessive and jealous. Adolescents may give your new partner a hard time. I highly advise keeping the physical affection low in front of children. Some children still hold on to the idea that their parents will eventually get back together. You might find your kids fighting for your attention as they will see your new partner as a rival.

Reassure your children that you have plenty of love to go around, and that they are the most important people in your life. Respect your kids' feelings and give them time to adjust. Tell your children this new person is not replacing their dad and that they only have one mom and one dad. When your partner becomes a part of your child's life, you need to discuss the rules of the family. You should discuss his participation in discipline and other important aspects of family life.

Be Yourself

I have learned the hard way to always be myself and not try to be what I think the man I am dating wants. Otherwise, they will not be falling in love with your true self, but rather a persona. This does nobody any good. I tend to be a chameleon. I need to focus on just being myself instead of trying to fit in or please someone.

Stories from the Dating Trenches

Now it's time for a good laugh. Here are some interesting dating stories from myself and other women. You will realize you aren't alone in this crazy thing called dating. Full names have been excluded to protect the guilty!

I was in another state just after leaving my husband of eight years. I was on the rebound, staying at a hotel in between two major cities. The hotel manager was cute and asked me out. I agreed to go. The first time we went out was to the Elks club for a dance and dinner to support local businesses. It was fun and I thought he was such a gentleman. I couldn't wait to spend more time with him. He walked me back up to my room and offered to hang for a bit. We watched a movie and I sent him home. I thought he was a great man and a lot of fun. Well, I was remarkably wrong. Fast-forward to our next date at a local bar. He got extremely drunk and kept falling to the floor. He was acting inappropriately and wound up getting into a bar fight! I ditched him for the night and found myself another cute man who was more respectable. ~Nicole, Stuart, Florida

Here's my story: Picture the guy taking you out on date and they forgot their wallet so you end up paying...then they call back for another date! Ah, no! No applications being accepted for broke dudes.
~Brittany, Jupiter, Florida

Several of my friends encouraged me to do the whole online dating thing. I was skeptical but I figured I would give it a try. What was interesting to me was before I even posted a photo I had tons of responses. None of the men appealed to me and a lot of them wrote odd or crude things. I finally decided to upload a photo of myself and then it got even more interesting. The first cute man who wrote to me seemed normal for about 20 minutes until he asked if I wore sexy heels. When I told him I was more of a flip-flop woman unless the occasion calls for heels, he told me I was not the one for him. Thankfully, I didn't waste any more time on him. I appreciate when men show their true colors right up front. The second man also seemed normal until he asked if there was a hotel by me and if I liked rough sex. Next. The last one asked for my e-mail address because he wanted to send me a picture of himself. Instead of sending his face he sent me a photo of his package. All I could think was gross! I didn't even respond to him. I quickly went to the dating site and deleted my profile. And that was the end of my online dating adventure. ~Andrea, Miller Place, New York

My husband and I met on the free online dating site called Plenty of Fish. After talking for about a month, we decided to meet in person at Borders Bookstore for tea and coffee. We had great conversation and then he asked me if I wanted to get something to eat. We decided to go to the diner down the road. As we started to approach the cars, he kept reaching into his pocket frantically. When I asked what was wrong, he told me he couldn't find his keys. We got to his car and it was locked. He looked in his window and his keys were hanging in the

189

ignition! It was hysterical and cute. He was so nervous about meeting for the first time that he forgot the keys in the ignition! I drove us to the diner. When we returned to the bookstore he had to call his dad to bring the spare key! He was embarrassed but I thought it was the cutest thing. His brother told this story during his best man speech at the wedding.   ~Kim, Ridge, New York

JR & I were set up on a blind date (Sept 1, 1978). We had never met each other but he knew my dad was quite financially successful & that I had been to lots of nice restaurants... He called me the week before we were supposed to go on the blind date to set up some of the specifics but he never told me where he was taking me for dinner. He lived in Hanford which was an hour and a half drive from my house in Bakersfield, California. He was quite late but called to apologize. Seems he had been gone for several weeks. He and his family were all dove hunting the morning of our date, and he forgot about the time! When he rang the doorbell, we talked for a minute and headed out to his parents' home for a FAMILY reunion... that was our first date! After dinner, he took me out to show me the little city where he lived, and as we approached his car he kissed me in front of his entire family. In 1978, I did not kiss anyone on the first date! Ha! Ten months later, we were married...that was 40 years ago! ~Charise, Port St. Lucie

After becoming separated from my husband at 42 years old, I imagined the dating world had to be a little different than the last time I was an active participant—about 14 years ago. I soon found out that it was A LOT different than I remembered, or could ever have imagined. I decided to try one of the free internet dating websites to see what it was all about. I set up an account, carefully filled out the profile and chose a few pictures to post. With nervous but excited anticipation I hit the button to begin my new foray into dating. By the next morning, I had about 20 messages from various men. This was a huge surprise as I have never thought of myself as one of those women who men found very attractive. It was completely overwhelming as well. As I started to read the messages, I became very confused, concerned that I had set up my account incorrectly. One of the first messages was from a man who simply asked. "Can I take you shoe shopping?" No "Hello, my name is..." He just wanted to buy me shoes. Although I LOVE shoes as much as the next girl, I blocked him and found out later from some of my newly made single mom friends that he approaches every woman with the same exact line.

Another message read "You are beautiful, do you want to f*ck?" I was taken aback. I weeded out a few more messages that were pretty much the same. Then I found a few that were, in my opinion, more normal than the rest. One man introduced himself, told me he found me very attractive and wanted to know if we could chat a little bit. I replied to him and we began to exchange messages. Around the fifth or sixth email from him, he asked me if I minded the fact that he was married and he was extremely unhappy and wanted a girlfriend. I replied to him that I am brand new to dating again and I really didn't want to start out this new chapter of my life being a homewrecker, and I blocked him.

Next, there was a really hot guy, and when I say hot, I mean like from a magazine hot, and I couldn't figure out why the hell he was messaging me! He was polite, introduced himself, and we began to chat. We then exchanged cell phone numbers. He asked me to send him a pic of myself, so I did, fully clothed. I didn't really know what sexting was yet but I was about to learn. He then sent me back a picture of his erect penis, then another and another. That was when I realized I stepped into the new bizzaro world of internet dating.

I have to tell you: My favorite messages came from guys who were young enough to be my son. These young men would tell me how inexperienced they were and how they would so very much like for an older (ugh, guys, never call a woman "older") woman to teach them *what to do and what women like. Basically, I think they wanted me to be a sex teacher or something. "Do this, don't do that, touch here, not there," the thought of it made me laugh. Although flattering (in a very off-putting way), I declined these messages as well.*

I did venture to meet a few internet men in real life and found that dating is backwards in this day and age (now I sound like my mother). From the people I met, the guy wants to have sex with you first then get to know you to see if they like you. Isn't it supposed to be the other way around? You get to know the person first and if you click then sex happens? I have to admit that if I just wanted to get some, and there were days that I did, this was an easy way to get it. It was like ordering sex, instead of Chinese food, for delivery but without the delivery charge. "Sure, I'll be there in 10 minutes." I have since closed my internet dating site account and decided that I would attempt to meet someone—when I am ready—the old-fashioned way, by going to a bar and getting drunk. ~Michelle, Coram, New York

Conclusion

You are a single mom ninja.

It's time for me to wrap up—my motherly duties and other life obligations are calling my name. It was a dream for me to write this book and I am proud of myself for accomplishing it. This book is like my second child. It took me a while to write it, but I finally gave birth to it! Thank you for taking the time to read it. I truly hope it has helped you. My goal is to make you laugh, feel inspired and empowered, and help you to know that you are never alone in your journey.

If you have your own story of thriving as a single mom and would like to be featured in my next book, send your story to info@slayingitbooks.com.

We are building a huge community of single moms slaying it, so join the tribe by visiting Single Mom Slaying It on Facebook at facebook.com/SingleMomSlayingIt, Sisterhood of Single Moms and Sisterhood Evolution!

We can't wait to meet you and hear your story.

My faith in myself, in the future, and in God keeps me going. My story is not over yet. I am only in the middle! I'd love to include another child into my home; only time will tell what will happen. I try to stay optimistic that good things are coming my way and encourage you to do the same! #slayingit #mamaslay

If this book has touched you in some way, help a fellow single momma out and recommend it to anyone you can think of who can benefit from reading. I would greatly appreciate you sharing this book with others. If you liked what you read, you can also write up positive reviews online so others can benefit from reading it. Thank you!

I wish you much happiness, strength, and confidence in your crazy single mom adventures. Realize that one day all your hard work and efforts will pay off. Your adult children will appreciate and thank you.

Namaste.

About the Author

Andrea M. Pearson is a Single Mom, Entrepreneur, Certified Personal Trainer, Certified Aerobics Instructor, and Women's Health & Life Coach. She runs Single Mom Slaying It and Sisterhood of Single Moms on Facebook and is the co-founder of Sisterhood Evolution.

Andrea's passions are fitness, wellness and health. She loves inspiring women to be the best they can be, and posts daily on her motivational pages on Facebook. Andrea lives life to the fullest—and makes the most of every single day that she is blessed to be on this beautiful earth. She truly enjoys uplifting others and being a positive friend and resource to many. Her favorite "job" has been being a mom. She hopes her journey as a single mom can help and inspire others.

Connect with Andrea online:

www.sisterhoodevolution.com
www.slayingitbooks.com
www.thehappinessroute.com
Facebook.com/AndreaPearsonCoaching
Facebook.com/SingleMomSlayingIt
Instagram.com/andreapearsoncoaching
Twitter.com/AndreaPearsonHC
Linkedin.com/in/andrea-pearson-563742111

Appendix A: Book List

Here are some great books I recommend for amazing single moms like you!

1. **Like She Owns the Place** by Cara Alwill Leyba

2. **Girl, Wash Your Face** by Rachel Hollis

3. **Radical Acceptance** by Tara Brach

4. **The Bravest You** by Adam Kirk Smith

5. **The Gift of Our Compulsions** by Mary O'Malley

6. **The Body Keeps the Score** by Bessel Van Der Kolk

7. **The Power of Habit** by Charles Duhigg

8. **The Compound Effect** by Darren Hardy

9. **Who Moved My Cheese?** by Spencer Johnson

10. **The Slight Edge** by Jeff Olson

11. **The Law of Attraction** by Esther and Jerry Hicks

12. **Eat Pray Love** by Elizabeth Gilbert

13. **Change Your Thoughts – Change Your Life** by Dr. Wayne W. Dyer

14. **Make Your Bed** by Admiral William McRaven

15. **Grit** by Angela Duckworth

16. **The Big Leap** by Gay Hendricks

17. **Rich Dad Poor Dad** by Robert Kiyosaki

18. Anything written by Tony Robbins, Jack Canfield, Napoleon Hill, Steven Covey, Eckhart Tolle, or Dale Carnegie

Appendix B: Additional Financial Advice from a Certified Financial Planner

Have you ever stopped to think about what your Human Life Value is? What do I mean by that? You are providing an income to your household. How much will that potentially be over your lifetime or at least your working years? What do you have in place to protect that income? What if you became sick or injured? Maybe you've never given any thought to this. You may be lucky enough to have an employer who offers disability insurance or life insurance as a benefit. Is it enough and how long could your family survive? What if you didn't die and had a debilitating disease that wouldn't allow you to continue working? Now you no longer have those employer benefits. At that point, you can't get disability insurance and may not likely qualify for life insurance either. It's always smart to have a personal policy that at least supplements what you have through work.

Disability Insurance

Let's separate out disability insurance for a moment. First of all, no disability policy is going to replace 100% of your income. If you have an employer disability insurance policy, make sure you look at how the premium is being paid. If it is being taken out pre-tax and you encounter a disability, the benefit will be taxable to you. Most employer disability policies replace somewhere between 50-66% of your pay. So, if you have a 60% disability income replacement policy and are in the 15% tax bracket, you will receive 45% of your pay. I'm sure if you're just making it on 100%, 60% is going to be a stretch, let alone 45%! Look to see if your employer allows the premium to be taken post tax. If you have this option and elect it, when you receive the benefit it will be tax-free.

Life Insurance

What if your company offers life insurance, do you still need your own personal policy? Most of us will not be working for the same company for our entire careers and even if we think we'd like to, the employer may have different plans for us. I can honestly say that this happened to me with my first "real" job out of college. I worked for a great employer, but one day I was out of a job. It can happen to anyone at any time. So how much life insurance do any of us need? To answer that question, you have to ask yourself: "What do I want it to do if I die prematurely?" The obvious is usually to cover final expenses, whether that's burial or cremation. Beyond that do you want it to pay off your debts if you have any? Do you want it to create an emergency fund for your family? Do you desire to fund your children's college or higher education? Do you want it to replace your income and for how long? Do you want to continue a tithe to your church upon your death?

By purchasing your own life insurance policy, you are also locking in future insurability. This means that if later you are diagnosed with a health issue that would otherwise make you uninsurable you don't have to worry because you already have life insurance. Plus, it's never going to be cheaper than it is right now (you will never be younger than you are today).

Be sure when you are shopping that you find a highly rated company. You can check any company's rating on www.ambest.com. AM Best is an independent rating agency that rates all insurance companies. This is important because you want to be sure that the company will be around to pay out the claim when your family needs it.

There are many different types of life insurance. There is term and permanent. The least expensive type of life insurance is term insurance. This type of life insurance will pay out "if" you die within the specified term. These are typically 10, 15, 20, or 30-year policies. There are also policies that have conversion provisions. What that means is if you later become uninsurable you could convert the policy to a permanent policy. There are two general types of permanent policies. They are Universal Life and Whole Life. Neither is necessarily better than the other. They are just different. Permanent policies all build cash value. Permanent policies from some expert mainstream financial gurus have gotten a bad rap. All I will say about that is if you believe theory is always realistic than believe the expert mainstream financial gurus.

I happen to be a realist and speak from my experience as a financial professional who has been helping people for nearly 10 years. Universal Life in its simplest form has cash value that earns an interest rate. Because of this the premium may have to be adjusted up or down over the life of the policy. Whole life policies pay dividends, although dividends are not guaranteed. I won't elaborate much more on the minute details of permanent life insurance because the most important thing it to have life insurance regardless of the type. No beneficiary that I've ever provided a check to has asked me what kind of life insurance, but they always care about the amount. Get what you can afford.

Auto Insurance

If you drive and own a car, you'll need auto insurance. I tell my clients to shop around about once a year when your policy is up for renewal. Find an agent who can provide multiple quotes; however, you may also want to check with other companies that don't use independent agents (i.e. State Farm). Make sure you understand your auto policy. Know what your deductibles are. Once you have a well-established emergency fund, you may want to raise your deductibles if it makes sense (cost-wise). Also, the most expensive part of auto insurance is for medical purposes. If you are in an accident and either you or the person involved in the accident needs medical care, you want to be sure you have enough coverage. Make sure you talk to your agent and understand the coverage you are paying for.

Homeowner's Insurance

If you own a home, you'll need homeowner's insurance. Again, shop around for this. If you rent, you'll want to consider renter's insurance. If the rental home burns to the ground, your landlord cannot legally cover your contents. They are only required to have insurance on the structure.

Health Insurance

The easiest way to bankrupt yourself is by not having health insurance. Hopefully if you are working, your employer will offer you group health insurance. This is by far the cheapest way to be covered. If you do not have this benefit, you'll need to shop the open market. Your employer may offer different types of plans (i.e. PPO, HMO, premium plans, high deductible plans, etc.). Look all the plans over when you are eligible to enroll.

If your family is healthy, you may want to consider a high deductible plan in order to save money on a per pay period basis. You can take the extra savings and put some or all of it into a Health Savings Account (HSA). An HSA is money that goes into an account on a pre-tax basis and can be used for medical expenses including co-pays, prescriptions, out-of-pocket expenses. The great part about HSAs is that the money rolls over from year to year unlike a flexible spending account. Note if you take money from the HSA for non-medical reasons you'll incur a 20% tax penalty and have to pay income taxes.

If you do not have a high deductible medical insurance option, the next best thing is to contribute to a flexible spending account and dependent care account depending on your situation. If you can elect to participate in a flexible spending account, the money you designate goes into the account on a pre-tax basis each pay period. As long as you have eligible expenses, you can get this money back. Be aware though with this type of account, if you have not used the money in the plan year, you will forfeit the money. Plan accordingly. Dependent care works in a similar fashion except it will reimburse you for eligible child care expenses.

Saving for Retirement

Once you have your emergency fund established and your debts paid off, you need to get serious about saving for retirement. There are many investment vehicles and options when it comes to putting away money for retirement. If you are lucky enough to work for an employer that has a 401k/403b and matches, be sure to take advantage of the matching funds. This is free money! Above the match, you'll want to see how many funds are available and what the costs are. Also find out if they offer a Roth option. I love Roth 401k's, 403b's, IRAs. Think about it this way: If you were a farmer and took some seed and planted a crop, would you want the tax deduction on the seed and have to pay taxes on the crop once it produces OR would you want to pay taxes on the seed and the entire crop be tax free once it produces? I'll take the latter all day long.

Saving for College

If funding your children's college education is important, you'll want to start putting money into an investment once your retirement is being well-funded. I have clients that have these two mixed up and I remind them that if they put their child through college with no loans, their child will not be supporting them in retirement. Again, I go back to the flight attendant analogy with the loss of cabin pressure and putting on your mask first.

Long-Term Care Insurance

As you start building wealth, you'll want to consider long-term care insurance to protect your assets. The one thing that you cannot predict is your future health. I've seen many clients caring for spouses, parents, and/or children because their family members did not purchase long-term care insurance. It's exhausting and not a situation I wish upon anyone. With higher incidence of dementia, Alzheimer's, Parkinson's, cancer, and diabetes, it's important to get this while you're healthy and not wait too long. By not having long-term care insurance you'll have to use your own assets, usually at an accelerated rate, and that can cause extra taxation. If you cannot pay for your own care, you'll have to seek the assistance of Medicaid, which is a long process and the result is you are a ward of the state. Your options are very limited and not a situation you want to be in.

Help is Available

You may be feeling a bit overwhelmed by all of this and that's normal. I would highly suggest seeking the help of a financial advisor. Ask someone you know who is financially successful, or who you know has a financial advisor. Make sure you research and/or go interview several advisors. Don't feel you have to settle on the first person you call or meet with. Ask how they work with their clients and how they are paid. If they are not clear about this, find another advisor. Find an advisor who cares about you and isn't just trying to sell you a product. They should stress the relationship and not just the sale. Make sure they get to know you and find out what your goals are.

A planner is someone who can give you quotes on insurance and help you with investments. A good indication that they are a skilled financial planner is they will have the initials CFP after their name. CFP stands for Certified Financial Planner. This is an advisor whose knowledge is better than the average. They have taken a number of financial courses and passed the CFP exam. They have taken an oath to abide by a fiduciary standard.

Legal Documents

Another important piece of your financial picture is having your legal documents in place. These are things like a will, power of attorney, medical directive, etc. You can have this done by an estate attorney or you can do it on your own. There are many online services to choose from. Just make sure if you do this that you follow the laws of your state so when it's time to use the documents that they are enforceable. You'll also want to be sure that all your bank accounts and investments have a named beneficiary.

Once you have done all of the above, you will be so far ahead of the typical American. You will be at a point where you can give like you've never given before. This is an awesome feeling!

Hopefully you figured giving to some degree in your initial budget, but what I'm talking about here is really making an impact. I know each one of you reading this is capable of doing everything I've talked about. It requires determination, persistence, and discipline. When you achieve this, you'll be living the American dream. Best of luck!

~Amy Whitlach, Thrivent Financial,
Amy.Whitlach@Thrivent.com

13684748R00120